Marxism, History
& Social~~ist Consci~~

By David N~~orth~~

Mehring Books
Oak Park, Michigan

ISBN 978-1-893638-03-7

Published by Mehring Books
P.O. Box 48377
Oak Park, MI 48237

Printed in the United States of America

Contents

Foreword

In May 2006 two former members of the Workers League (predecessor of the Socialist Equality Party), Alex Steiner and Frank Brenner, published a critique of the theoretical work, political line and practical activity of the International Committee of the Fourth International. Entitled *Objectivism or Marxism*[1], the document was unsparing in its criticism of what its authors perceived to be the moribund state of political and intellectual life within the International Committee. Given the fact that nearly three decades had elapsed since the authors had resigned from the Workers League and abandoned active revolutionary socialist politics, the International Committee was under no special obligation to respond to the criticisms of Steiner and Brenner. However, as has so often been the case in the past, the criticism provided an opportunity to clarify important issues of revolutionary history, Marxist theory and socialist program. The most compelling reason for preparing an extensive reply was that the Steiner-Brenner document was a veritable compendium of pseudo-Marxist and essentially reactionary conceptions popular among petty-bourgeois radicals influenced by various schools of thought associated with the Frankfurt School and con-

---

1   The document can be accessed at *http://www.permanent-revolution.org*.

temporary neo-utopianism. The document presented in this volume, *Marxism, History and Socialist Consciousness*, originally published on June 28, 2006 [and circulated among the members and supporters of the Socialist Equality Party and the International Committee], is the reply of the International Committee to the Steiner-Brenner document.

Exactly one year has passed since *Marxism, History and Socialist Consciousness* was dispatched via email to Steiner and Brenner. The receipt of this document was noted on their web site, along with the observation that it "deserved a careful and considered reply." However, proclaiming that "Nothing less than the future of the revolutionary movement depends on it," Steiner and Brenner warned that they "would not be rushed." At least in this they have been true to their word. Their reply, on which we have been told that so much depends, has yet to see the light of day.

But the world moves on. And while it is possible that Steiner and Brenner may yet bring their belated magnum opus to fruition, it seems to us that something akin to a statute of limitations has been passed. There is no reason for us to wait any longer in bringing *Marxism, History and Socialist Consciousness* to the attention of a broader public interested in Marxist theory. It is my hope that this document will prove helpful in illuminating the profound and unbridgeable chasm between Marxism and various contemporary forms of petty-bourgeois radical ideology.

David North
Detroit
June 28, 2007

Marxism, History & Socialist Consciousness

1. Introduction

Dear Comrades Steiner and Brenner:

The International Committee of the Fourth International (ICFI) has asked that I reply to your document, "Objectivism or Marxism," on its behalf. This is a task that I undertake with a certain degree of regret. Notwithstanding the different paths our lives have taken over the past three decades, I retain warm recollections of the time when we worked closely together within the movement. However, that was very long ago, and your latest document serves only to underscore what your various writings over the past several years have made increasingly apparent: that you have traveled very far politically from Marxism, the political heritage of the Trotskyist movement, and the ICFI. This inescapable political reality must determine the content and the tone of this reply.

Your letter begins by protesting that the ICFI has failed to answer your previous documents, from which you draw the most disturbing conclusions: The ICFI suffers from "an aversion to criticism" that is "symptomatic of deeper problems within the movement that every member and supporter of the IC should be concerned about." The leadership of the movement "stonewalls political debate," and seeks "to quell discussion in order to insulate itself from criticism." Our alleged failure to respond to your documents "only underscores how alien a practice genuinely critical debate has become within the movement."

To the uninformed observer, the situation you describe can only evoke images of a besieged opposition tendency in a dictatorial political party, battling against a bureaucratic regime's suppression of its democratic right to be heard by the rank-and-file membership. The reality, as you both know, is radically different. Neither of you is a member of the Socialist Equality Party (SEP). You have been out of the movement for just short of 28 years.[1] This does count for something. You refer to your "long histories *with* the movement" – a description that is self-consciously ambiguous. There is a difference between "with" and "within." For most of your adult lives, you have not been members of the party. The mere fact that you have maintained cordial relations with the movement does not obligate us to respond to your documents as we would to those of members of the SEP or other sections of the ICFI.

No one in the ICFI is stopping you from criticizing the policies and program of our movement, and posting what you write on your own web site for all to read (to the extent that you are willing to moderate what appears to be your rejection of the internet as a fully-legitimate mode of political communication). You are free to gather the support of like-minded individuals and campaign for your views. In turn, the ICFI and the SEP are well within their political rights to reply or not to your documents as we see fit. It is not our responsibility to provide you with a forum for a perspective that opposes the traditions and program of the Fourth International. In submitting this reply to your public criticisms, the ICFI is not fulfilling a "legal" responsibility, but making clear the deep and fundamental differences between Marxian

---

1   Comrade Steiner, you left the Workers League in September 1978, and Comrade Brenner, you resigned in January 1979.

socialism and the pseudo-utopianism – a form of middle-class ideology – that you, Comrades Steiner and Brenner, espouse.

2. The International Committee and the *World Socialist Web Site*

Although you have not been members of our movement for almost three decades, and have no knowledge of its internal life, you make the most sweeping accusations against the International Committee. You assert that there is "a disturbing absence of organized theoretical or political discussion within the movement." On what is this claim based? Other than your displeasure with the manner in which we have dealt with your documents, how has this theoretical and political decay manifested itself in our political line? This is a question that you do not address. Even if one were to admit the possibility that the ICFI failed to give your documents the attention they merited, this error would not by itself rise to the level of a world-historical event. It is still necessary for you to demonstrate that there exists a connection between your complaint and more serious political problems relating to world developments external to yourselves. It is not sufficient for you to assert that a connection exists. You must prove it, and the way this has been done in the history of the Marxist movement is through a careful and exhaustive analysis of the political line of the organization that is the subject of the criticism.

If you had chosen to proceed in this theoretically principled manner, there is no shortage of materials upon which you would be able to draw. The last 20 years have witnessed colossal changes: in technology, the structure of world capitalism, the relation of national states to the global economy, and, let us not forget, the political geography of the world. Maps printed 20 years ago are now useless. All of these interrelated processes – technological, economic and political – have had a profound impact on the international class struggle. The response of the International Committee to these historic changes would easily fill up several dozen volumes.

However, nowhere in your document is there to be found any analysis of, or even reference to, the political line of the International Committee. One does not even find the words "Iraq War," "Bush administration," "September 11th," "China," "Afghanistan," "Iran," "terror," or "globalization." These are not careless omissions. You are not interested in political analysis and perspectives, at least as these concerns have been under- stood historically in the Fourth International. *Quite the oppo- site: you believe that the International Committee's concentration on Marxist political analysis and commentary is itself a funda- mental mistake. You vehemently reject the conception that such analysis and commentary, based on the method of historical ma- terialism, is essential or even relevant to the development of social- ist consciousness.* This position underlies your bitter hostility toward the *World Socialist Web Site*, which you consider to be the main expression of all that you believe wrong with the International Committee.

You write that "for all intents and purposes the International Committee has ceased to function." On what is this conclusion based? "It is hard even to recall the last time the International Committee held a meeting in its own name. For years now virtually all the authoritative statements of the movement have been issued as *WSWS* statements, and now the gather- ing in Australia – which was clearly an international confer- ence of the movement – is presented not in the name of a revolutionary party but rather in that of an editorial board of a web site."

That is not all. You ask: "Was the morphing of the IC into the *WSWS* ever discussed or voted on at a party conference?" And "Where is the document that explains to the working class public the reasons for such an important shift? How is it possible to square the repeated proclamations of internationalism with the mothballing of the organizational expression of revolutionary internationalism?"

You speak of the "morphing of the IC into the *WSWS*" as if there were something illegitimate and underhanded in the founding of the latter. In this regard, your attack closely parallels the response of the Spartacist League to the establishment of the *World Socialist Web Site*.[2] However, nowhere do you claim that the founding of the *WSWS* involved a change in the political line of the International Committee. The *World Socialist Web Site*, as its masthead explicitly states, is published by the International Committee. While you may be in doubt about the political connection of the ICFI to the *World Socialist Web Site*, it is not a secret to its thousands of daily readers. Moreover, since the days of Marx's *Neue Rheinische Zeitung*, the theoretical and programmatic identity of a revolutionary tendency has been synonymous with the name of its publication. We might include in our list the *Neue Zeit* of the revolutionary German Social Democratic Party, the *Iskra*, *Vperyod* and *Pravda* of the Leninists, the *Bulletin* of the anti-Stalinist opposition in the U.S.S.R., *The Militant* and, later, *The Socialist Appeal* of the Trotskyists in the United States during the late 1920s and 1930s, *The Newsletter* produced by the British Trotskyists working inside the British Labour Party, and even the *Bulletin* of the Workers League. We have

---

2   The Robertson group wrote in March 1998: "The new SEP Web site, rapidly expanding via the gaseous 'great Thoughts' of David North, is the latest in a growing junk belt of virtual fantasy worlds, where posturing little grey men with gigantic egos and dubious politics can play at revolution. . . . To pretend dumping some documents into cyberspace is any substitute for the hard fight——in the real world, among real people——to build a revolutionary workers party, only confirms the total depths of cynicism and humbug for which the Northites are infamous."

no reason to be troubled by the fact that the *World Socialist Web Site* is looked to by thousands of readers as the authentic voice of socialist internationalism.

Your suggestion that the *WSWS* was somehow established behind the back of the ICFI is absurd on its face. Yes, there was a public statement issued on the founding of the *World Socialist Web Site*, which you can still access if you are interested.[3] And, since you have asked, the founding of the *WSWS* was indeed preceded by an intensive discussion spanning almost one year within every section of the ICFI. How else would it have been possible to mobilize the high level of active support and participation by the cadre that has sustained daily publication of the *WSWS* for the last eight and a half years? Since the founding of the *WSWS* in February 1998, more than 18,000 articles have been published by an international editorial board that directs the collective work of a constantly-expanding cadre of Marxist writers assembled on the basis of the principles, history, theoretical outlook and perspective of the International Committee. In both theory and practice, the *WSWS* represents a historic milestone in the development of revolutionary internationalism. Your political blindness, exacerbated by personal subjectivism, leads you to speak of the "mothballing of the organizational expression of revolutionary internationalism" at a time when the ICFI is directing the daily publication of a web site that provides commentary in 13 languages: English, French, German, Italian, Spanish, Portuguese, Russian, Polish, Serbo-Croatian, Turkish, Sinhalese, Tamil and Indonesian. If this represents in your mind the end "for all intents and purposes" of the International Committee, one can only wonder what you think constitutes real international activity? Three decades ago, when you were still members of the movement, the internal life of the ICFI consisted of little more than occasional visits by representatives of affiliated or sympathizing sections to the offices of the WRP in London. Cliff Slaughter, the nominal secretary of the ICFI, maintained no regular contact with the international cadre. There was no systematic discussion, let alone collaboration, on the perspective of the International Committee. To the extent that your conception of internationalism was shaped in the era of the extreme degeneration of Healy's organization, it is simply impossible for either of you to conceive of what it is to work in a movement whose daily political activity entails the most intense international collaboration.

3. The International Editorial Board and the perspectives of the ICFI

During the past year the International Committee sponsored two major theoretical and political projects: first, the series of nine lectures on "Marxism, the October Revolution and the Historical Foundations of the Fourth International" that were delivered in Ann Arbor, Michigan, August 14-20, 2005; second, the meeting of the International Editorial Board of the *World Socialist Web Site*, held in Sydney, Australia, January 22-27, 2006. Your reaction to these events is a devastating self-exposure of your abandonment of Marxism and hostility to the political outlook and traditions of the Trotskyist movement.

We are not surprised by your angry response to the reports and lectures delivered at these meetings. Notwithstanding your official "protest" over the ICFI's alleged failure to respond to your documents, you quite clearly recognized that the theoretical conceptions and perspective elaborated in the presentations represented an unequivocal repudiation of your campaign to infiltrate the disoriented anti-Marxist pseudo-utopianism of Wilhelm Reich, Ernst Bloch and Herbert Marcuse into the

Fourth International – that is, to fundamentally change the theoretical and programmatic foundations and class orientation of the Trotskyist movement. That is what you are actually referring to when you write that "the substance of the lectures and reports issued from these gatherings [does not] suggest any new openness to critical debate."

You describe the editorial board reports as "more a simulacrum of a perspectives document than the real thing: they are less a guide to revolutionary practice than a version of Foreign Affairs with a Marxist coloration. They are indeed *editorial board* reports – i.e., perspectives for more journalism. The question of what is to be done hardly enters into them at all, aside from ritualistic statements at the end about the need to build the revolutionary party. In other words, the essence of a revolutionary perspective is missing in these reports, but this is the very thing the IC refuses to discuss."

That is the sum total of what you have to say about the reports delivered at the editorial board meeting. There is no analysis of the material that was actually presented. Your indifference to the content of the reports – which collectively represented the most comprehensive examination of the world political situation ever presented at a gathering of the International Committee since its founding in 1953 – provides the key to an understanding of your own political outlook and class standpoint.

Let us review the content of the IEB meeting that you so contemptuously dismiss as a "simulacrum of a perspectives document…" What you are rejecting is the effort of the International Committee to establish the *objective* foundations, based on a comprehensive and integrated analysis of the world political and economic situation, of the prospects for socialist revolution. The approach taken by the IEB to the development of world revolutionary perspectives is best explained by presenting a lengthy citation from my opening report:

Any serious attempt at a political prognosis, at an estimate of the potentialities within the existing political situation, must proceed from a precise and accurate understanding of the historical development of the world capitalist system.

The analysis of the historical development of capitalism must answer the following essential question: Is capitalism as a world economic system moving along an upward trajectory and still approaching its apogee, or is it in decline and even plunging toward an abyss?

The answer that we give to this question has, inevitably, the most far-reaching consequences, not only for our selection of practical tasks, but for the entire theoretical and programmatic orientation of our movement. It is not a subjective desire for social revolution that determines our analysis of the historical condition of the world capitalist system. Rather, the revolutionary perspective must be rooted in a scientifically-grounded assessment of the objective tendencies of socio-economic development. Detached from the necessary objective socio-economic prerequisites, a revolutionary perspective can be nothing more than a utopian construction.

How, then, do we understand the present stage of capitalism's historical development? Let us consider two opposed conceptions. The Marxist position is, as we know, that the world capitalist system is at an advanced stage of crisis – indeed, that the outbreak of the world war in 1914, followed by the Russian Revolution in 1917, represented a fundamental turning point in world history. The convulsive events of the more than three decades between the outbreak of the First World War and the conclusion of the Second World War in 1945 demonstrated that capitalism had outlived its historic mission, and that the objective prerequisites for the socialist transformation of world economy had emerged. That capitalism had survived the crisis of those decades was, to a very great extent, the product of the failure and betrayals of the leaderships of the mass parties and organizations of the working class, above all the Social-Democratic and Communist parties and trade unions. Without their betrayals, the restabilization of world capitalism after World War II – drawing on the still substantial resources of the United States – would not have been possible. Indeed, despite the post-war stabilization, the global opposition of the working class and oppressed masses in the old colonial regions to capitalism and imperialism persisted; but its revolutionary potential was suppressed by the old bureaucratic organizations.

Finally, the betrayal and defeats of the mass struggles of the 1960s and 1970s cleared the way for a capitalist counter-offensive. The economic processes and technological changes that made possible the unprecedented global integration of the capitalist system shattered the old working class organizations, based on national perspectives and policies. The collapse of the Stalinist regimes in the Soviet Union and Eastern Europe – based on the bankrupt anti-Marxist program of a nationalistic pseudo-socialism – was the outcome of this process.

Despite the rapid territorial expansion of capitalism in the 1990s, the historical crisis persisted and deepened. The processes of globalization that had proved fatal to the old labor movements raised to an unprecedented level of tension the contradiction between the globally integrated character of capitalism as a world economic system and the nation-state structure within which capitalism is historically rooted and from which it cannot escape. The essentially insoluble character of this contradiction – or, at least, its "insolubility" on any progressive basis – finds daily expression in the mounting disorder and violence that characterizes the present world situation. A new period of revolutionary upheaval has begun. That, very briefly, is the Marxist analysis.

What is the alternative perspective? Let us consider the following counter-hypothesis:

What the Marxists, to use Leon Trotsky's florid phrase, termed the "death agony of capitalism" was, rather, its violent and protracted birth pangs. The various socialist and revolutionary experiments of the twentieth century were not merely premature, but essentially utopian. The history of the twentieth century should be read as the story of capitalism overcoming all obstacles to the inexorable triumph of the market as the supreme system of economic organization. The fall of the Soviet Union and the turn of China to market economics represented the culmination of this process. This decade and, in all likelihood, the decade that follows will continue to witness the rapid expansion of capitalism throughout Asia. The most significant element of this process will be the emergence of China and India as mature and stable world capitalist powers.

Moreover, if this hypothesis is correct, we may assume that within 20 years or so capitalism will enter—in accordance with the paradigm of W.W. Rostow—its 'takeoff' stage in Africa and the Middle East. Countries such as Nigeria, Angola, South Africa, Egypt, Morocco and Algeria (and/or perhaps others) will experience explosive economic growth. Thus, during the next half century—perhaps even in time for academic observances of the 200th anniversary in 2047 (only 41 years from now) of the publication of Karl Marx's and Friedrich Engels' *Communist Manifesto*—the global triumph of world capitalism will be completed and secured.

Does this hypothesis offer a realistic basis for the understanding of contemporary global processes? If it does, then there is little that is left of the Marxist revolutionary perspective. We would not be obligated to renounce our concern for the conditions of the working class. Indeed, there would be no shortage of conditions to be concerned about. We would attempt to formulate a program of minimum demands to improve the conditions of the world's poor and exploited. This, however, would be, to some extent, an exercise in social philanthropy. For erstwhile Marxists would be obligated to recognize the utopian character of the revolutionary project—at least for the historically foreseeable future. And they would be compelled to revise substantially their understanding of the past.

But is the hypothesis—of a globally triumphant capitalism—realistic? Is it reasonable, in light of all previous historical experience, to imagine a set of conditions that would allow the world capitalist system to resolve, or at least contain, the many potentially explosive problems already visible on the economic and political horizon before they threaten the very existence of the existing world order?

Do we consider it likely that geo-political and economic conflicts between the major world powers, within the framework of the imperialist system, will be resolved on the basis of negotiation and multi-lateral agreements before these disputes reach, and even pass beyond, the point at which they profoundly destabilize international politics?

Is it probable that disputes over access to and control of raw materials critical for economic development—especially, but not limited to, oil and natural gas—can be settled without violent conflict?

Will the innumerable struggles for regional influence—such as that between China and Japan or China and India for a dominant position in Asia—be resolved without resort to arms?

Is it likely that the United States can continue to pile up current accounts deficits to the tune of trillions of dollars without fundamentally destabilizing the global economy? And can the world economy absorb without significant financial turmoil the impact of a major economic crisis in the United States?

Will the United States be prepared to retreat from its hegemonic aspirations and accept a more egalitarian distribution of global power among states? Will it be prepared to yield ground, on the basis of compromise and concessions, to economic and potential military competitors, whether in Europe or in Asia?

Will the United States graciously and peacefully accommodate the rising influence of China?

On the social front, will the staggering rise in social inequality throughout North America, Europe and Asia continue without generating significant and even violent levels of social conflict? Does the political and social history of the United States support the view that the American working class will accept for years and decades to come, without substantial and bitter protest, a continuing downward spiral of its living standards?

These are the sorts of questions that must be answered before concluding that world capitalism has entered upon a new Golden Age of expansion and stability.

Those who would answer all the above questions in the affirmative are placing heavy bets against the lessons of history.

In the course of the coming week, these questions will be addressed.

In conclusion, I briefly explained the analytical method that guided the International Editorial Board:

> The main task to which we will devote ourselves this week is to provide an outline of the main features of the rapidly developing crisis of the world capitalist system.
>
> Lenin wrote in 1914 that "The splitting of a single whole and the cognition of its contradictory parts . . . is the *essence* (one of the 'essentials,' one of the principal, if not the principal, characteristics or features) of dialectics."
>
> In accordance with this theoretical approach, the reports that we will hear will examine from various sides and aspects the development of global crisis.

My opening remarks were followed by:

1. Nick Beams' report on the state of the world capitalist economy, which placed the present conjuncture within the context of the decisive and complex role of the United States in the global system during the 20th century.

2. James Cogan's analysis of "The consequences of the US-led war against Iraq."

3. Barry Grey's report on "The Bush administration and the global decline of US capitalism."

4. Patrick Martin's examination of "The social and political crisis of the United States and the 2006 SEP election campaign."

5. John Chan's study of "The implications of China for world socialism."

6. Ulrich Rippert's report on "The dead-end of European capitalism and the tasks of the working class."

7. Julie Hyland's presentation on "New Labour and the decay of democracy in Britain."

8. Bill Van Auken's report on "Latin American perspectives."

9. David Walsh's appraisal of "Artistic and cultural problems in the current situation."

10. Richard Hoffman's analysis of "Democratic rights and the attack on constitutionalism."

11. Wije Dias's report on "South Asia and the political bankruptcy of bourgeois nationalism and Stalinism."

12. Richard Tyler's examination of "Africa and the perspective of international socialism."

13. Jean Shaoul's analysis of "The economic, social and political disaster produced by the Zionist project."

You have nothing to say about any of the reports presented at the meeting of the International Editorial Board. You offer no response to the question that I posed in opening the IEB conference. You do not state whether you agree or disagree with the analyses presented by the reporters. Comrade Nick Beams offered a comprehensive review of the development of the world capitalist economy, placing particular emphasis on the disequilibrium within the world system and its far-reaching implications for both inter-imperialist relations and the international class struggle. This analysis forms a critical foundation for the perspective of the ICFI. What is the reason for your silence on this report? Comrade Cogan's report was devoted to the single most important international event: the American occupation of Iraq. Your document makes no reference to this report, nor do you raise the question of the war. Are you in agreement or disagreement with Cogan's analysis? Were I to continue down the list of reports, the same question would be repeated again and again. Why do you fail to ad-

dress concretely any aspect of the political analysis presented
by the ICFI in its extensive reports? Your non-response cannot be explained as mere indifference. What is involved here
is the outright rejection of the Marxist concept of perspective,
which strives to root revolutionary practice in as correct and
precise an analysis of the objective world as possible. As far as
you are concerned, this is simply a waste of time. You do not
believe that the type of reports given at the editorial board is
in any way related to the development of what you consider to
be "socialist consciousness." What you mean by that term, as
we shall explain in greater detail somewhat later, differs profoundly from the conception of revolutionary consciousness
that inspired the work of the best representatives of Marxism.
You want the International Committee to concern itself primarily not with politics and history, but with psychology
and sex – particularly as presented in the works of Wilhelm
Reich and Herbert Marcuse. These subjects are for you the
basis upon which "socialist consciousness" and "socialist idealism" should be constructed. That is why you respond with
cold indifference to the work conducted by the International
Editorial Board. Its attempt to elaborate a world revolutionary perspective, based on a study of the historically-developed
socio-economic and political contradictions of capitalism as a
global system, is rooted in a Marxist political tradition from
which you have become totally alienated.

4. Dialectics, pragmatism and
the theoretical work of the ICFI

The manner in which you deal with the other major theoretical project of the International Committee – the lectures
held last summer in Ann Arbor – is a travesty. Once again
you make no effort to address seriously and objectively the

content of the lectures. Of the nine lectures presented at the summer school, you ignore five. As for the four lectures that I delivered, you do not quote one complete sentence from any of them. The attacks that you make on my lectures generally involve distortions, gross simplifications or outright falsification of the positions I advanced. One is entitled to conclude that you assume that the audience for whom you are writing will not have read, or have any interest in reading, the actual text of the lectures.

You begin your critique of the summer school with the following statement:

> Dialectics is a dead letter in the IC. The movement hasn't produced a single article on dialectical philosophy in 20 years and no lecture was devoted to it at the summer school. Predictably enough, the abandonment of dialectics has also meant the abandonment of the struggle against pragmatism. The latter didn't rate so much as a single mention in any of the lectures. A telling instance of how invisible pragmatism has become in the IC's outlook is the fact that while Richard Rorty is discussed in one lecture as a representative postmodernist, his role as a prominent philosophical pragmatist is completely ignored. This is astonishing given that the struggle against pragmatism was at one time considered the most important element in the training of a conscious revolutionary leadership within the International Committee.

What a dishonest method of argumentation! You offer as proof of the death of dialectics in the ICFI and the abandonment of the fight against pragmatism our focus on Richard Rorty as a leading postmodernist, rather than on his role as a pragmatist. What is the point of such nonsense? Do you seriously believe that no one in the audience knew that Richard Rorty, America's most celebrated philosopher, is a pragmatist? Or that they were unaware that postmodernism is itself a major tendency within contemporary pragmatic philosophy. My discussion of Rorty, which extends for several pages, focused on the two theoretical questions that are central to the struggle against pragmatism: 1) Rorty's rejection of the possibility of objective knowledge and the concept of objective truth; and 2) his virulent rejection of the concept of history as an objective and law-governed process from which lessons can be drawn. In the course of my examination of Rorty, I stated:

> He proposes to banish from discussion the product of more than 200 years of social thought. Underlying this proposal is the conception that the development of thought itself is a purely arbitrary and largely subjective process. Words, theoretical concepts, logical categories, and philosophical systems are merely verbal constructs, *pragmatically* conjured up in the interest of various subjective ends. The claim that the development of theoretical thought is an objective process, expressing man's evolving, deepening, and ever-more complex and precise understanding of nature and society is, as far as Rorty is concerned, nothing more than a Hegelian-Marxian shibboleth.

Is this not, Comrades Steiner and Brenner, a concise and correct explanation of an essential conflict between Marxism and pragmatism?

To the extent that your indictment of my supposed failure to deal with pragmatism is not merely a factionally-motivated distortion but also an expression of your own theoretical conceptions, your casual treatment of the question of postmodernism is not without significance. You write that

The assumption that postmodernism has replaced pragmatism and empiricism as the principal ideological threat to Marxism is deeply misguided. Postmodernism is an academic fad that gained currency out of the rightward shift of the generation of Sixties radicals and the incorporation of many of them into the upper middle class. By contrast, pragmatism and empiricism are bound up with the entire historic development of Western capitalism. ... Moreover postmodernism is by now very much a fad on the wane. Many of its principal spokesmen have either passed away or gone into retirement and those who remain active often find themselves on the defensive, with condemnations of postmodernism now commonplace in radical and liberal circles. Twenty years ago it would have mattered to mount an attack on postmodernism; today it is an exercise in flogging, if not a dead horse, at least a very puny one.

This is a superficial, impressionistic and unserious approach to the examination of philosophical tendencies. First of all, I have nowhere stated or even implied that postmodernism has *replaced* pragmatism. It is, rather, a variety of pragmatic thought – indeed, one that takes the subjective idealist, voluntarist and even irrational elements that are present in classical pragmatic thought – dating all the way back to James – to their most extreme and reactionary conclusion. To suggest, as your comment does, that postmodernism represents a fundamentally different species of theoretical thought is to make a major concession to pragmatism, to shield pragmatism from the intellectual embarrassment it suffers on account of the gross excesses of its postmodernist progeny.

Similarly, to refer to postmodernism as "a fad on the wane" is to make light of a philosophical tendency that is a significant expression of both the reactionary character and deep crisis of bourgeois thought. A petty-bourgeois academic, who flits from one half-baked conception to another, may describe postmodernism as a "fad," especially as he prepares to jump on some new intellectual bandwagon without bothering to give a proper accounting of his last philosophical escapade. But that is not how a Marxist appraises the significance of a theoretical trend. What one or another subjective-idealist philosophical tendency calls itself is secondary. The main issue is its relationship to the history of philosophy. You correctly state that pragmatism and empiricism "are bound up with the entire history of Western capitalism." But is that not the case with postmodernism, which draws not only upon the American pragmatic traditions but also other deeply reactionary philosophical trends? Are there not deep and disturbing echoes of Kierkegaard, Schopenhauer, Nietzsche and Heidegger in the writings of contemporary postmodernists, including those of the pragmatist Richard Rorty?

5. How the ICFI has fought pragmatism

You assert that "Dialectics is a dead letter in the IC" and that we have abandoned the fight against pragmatism. You fail to explain precisely how that has manifested itself in the political line of our movement. We have not, you tell us, produced a single article on dialectical philosophy during the past 20 years. That statement, as a matter of fact, is not true.[4] But

---

4   The most recent essay on dialectical philosophy is my own detailed critique of *Marx After Marxism*, by Professor Tom Rockmore. [See "Hegel, Marx, Engels and the Origins of Marxism," http://wsws.org/articles/2006/may2006/rock-m02.shtml] This piece was published in the May 2-3, 2006 editions of the *World Socialist Web Site*, nearly two weeks

even if it were, it would still be necessary to demonstrate how the neglect of dialectics has expressed itself in the political analyses and work of the movement during this long period. Presumably, we have been working with some method. If, as you assert, the death of dialectics within the IC has been accompanied by the abandonment of the struggle against pragmatism, then the work of our movement has been dominated by the latter method. However, you make no attempt to substantiate that claim. In virtually every document that you write, you ritualistically invoke Trotsky's statement that "dialectical training of the mind is as necessary to a revolutionary fighter as finger exercises to a pianist." When Trotsky wrote these words, they carried the full force of the work of a political genius whose mastery of the dialectical method found incomparable expression in his brilliant analyses of world events. Unfortunately, when you use these words, it sounds more like a couch potato declaiming hypocritically on the importance of aerobics.

Trotsky did not simply tell Burnham and Shachtman that dialectics was important. He demonstrated how Burnham's pragmatism and Shachtman's agnostic attitude toward materialist dialectics were manifested in their analysis of the class nature of the Soviet state and their rejection of the defense of the U.S.S.R. against imperialist attack. In the 1939-40 struggle inside the Socialist Workers Party, the issue of dialectics was not introduced as a means of evading political questions, but in order to clarify them. As Trotsky wrote to Professor James Burnham, "it was not I but you who raised the question of the character of the U.S.S.R., thereby forcing me to pose the question of the method through which the class character of the state is determined." [*In Defense of Marxism* (London,

---

before you sent us your document. For reasons best known to yourselves, you chose to ignore it.

1971), p. 101] And as he further explained, "Correct method not only facilitates the attainment of a correct conclusion, but, connecting every new conclusion with the preceding conclusions in a consecutive chain, fixes the conclusions in one's memory. If political conclusions are made empirically, if inconsistency is proclaimed as a kind of advantage, then the Marxist system of politics is invariably replaced by impressionism – in so many ways characteristic of petty-bourgeois intellectuals. Every new turn of events catches the empiricist-impressionist unawares, compelling him to forget what he himself wrote yesterday, and produces a consuming desire for new formulae before new ideas have appeared in his head." [p. 73]

If Trotsky's criticism of the pragmatic method retains its validity, you should have no problem in demonstrating the inconsistencies and blunders in the political line of the ICFI over the past two decades. You present no such analysis. Thus, only two conclusions are possible: either method is not important as it has no discernable effect on the formulation of a political line; or your claim that we have abandoned dialectics and succumbed to pragmatism is a rhetorical flourish without any substance. We think that the second explanation is the correct one.[5]

---

5   The ICFI doesn't simply talk about the dialectical method. It seeks to apply it as an instrument of political analysis. For example, in a lecture on the nature of trade unionism given in Australia in 1998, I sought to demonstrate how dialectical logic sheds light on the nature of this complex social form:

> It must be kept in mind that when we set out to study trade unionism, we are dealing with a definite social form. By this, we mean not some sort of casual, accidental and amorphous collection of individuals, but rather a historically-evolved connection between people organized in classes and rooted in certain specific relations of production. It is also important to reflect upon the nature of

form itself. We all know that a relation exists between form and content, but this relationship is generally conceived as if the form were merely the expression of content. From this standpoint, the social form might be conceptualized as merely an outward, plastic and infinitely malleable expression of the relations upon which it is based. But social forms are more profoundly understood as dynamic elements in the historical process. To say that "content is formed" means that form imparts to the content of which it is the expression definite qualities and characteristics. It is through form that content exists and develops.

Perhaps it will be possible to clarify the purpose of this detour into the realm of philosophical categories and abstractions by referring to the famous section in the first chapter of the first volume of *Capital*, in which Marx asks: "Whence, then, arises the enigmatical character of the product of labor, so soon as it assumes the form of commodities? Clearly from the form itself." That is, when a product of labor assumes the form of a commodity – a transformation that occurs only at a certain stage of society – it acquires a peculiar, fetishistic quality that it did not previously possess. Once products are exchanged on the market, real social relations between people, of which commodities are themselves the outcome, necessarily assume the appearance of a relation between things. A product of labor is a product of labor; and yet, once it assumes, within the framework of new productive relations, the form of a commodity, it acquires new and extraordinary social properties.

Similarly, a group of workers is a group of workers. And yet, when that group assumes the form of a trade union, it acquires, through that form, new and quite distinct social properties to which the workers are inevitably subordinated. What, precisely, is meant by this? The trade unions represent the working class in a very distinct socio-economic role: as the seller of a commodity, labor power. Arising on the basis of the productive relations and property forms of capitalism, the essential purpose of the trade union is to secure for this commodity the best price that can be obtained under prevailing market conditions.

Of course, there is a world of difference between what I have described in theoretical terms as the "essential purpose" of trade unions and their real-life activities. The practical reality – the ev-

The source of your problem is that you do not understand, nor are you interested in, the relationship between method and revolutionary politics. It is one thing to declaim on the importance of dialectics and the fight against pragmatism. It is quite another to make this more than an abstract slogan – that is, to relate the struggle against pragmatism to the work of the party. While you somehow manage to acknowledge in your document that "North correctly defended dialectics from the distortions introduced by Healy," there is no indication in any of your various writings that you have actually studied the documents in which I exposed Healy's fraudulent use of Hegelian phraseology, or that you have assimilated the lessons of that crucial theoretical struggle. To no small extent this failing is to be explained by the fact that your departure from the movement preceded the development of the American

---

eryday sell-out of the most immediate interests of the working class – corresponds very little to the theoretically conceived "norm." This divergence does not contradict the theoretical conception, but is itself the outcome of the objective socio-economic function of the trade union. Standing on the basis of capitalist production relations, the trade unions are, by their very nature, compelled to adopt an essentially hostile attitude toward the class struggle. Directing their efforts toward securing agreements with employers that fix the price of labor power and determine the general conditions in which surplus-value will be pumped out of the workers, the trade unions are obligated to guarantee that their members supply their labor-power in accordance with the terms of the negotiated contracts. As Gramsci noted, "The union represents legality, and must aim to make its members respect that legality."

The defense of legality means the suppression of the class struggle, which, in the very nature of things, means that the trade unions ultimately undermine their ability to achieve even the limited aims to which they are officially dedicated. Herein lies the contradiction upon which trade unionism flounders. [*Marxism and the Trade Unions*, accessible on the *World Socialist Web Site* at http://www.wsws.org/exhibits/unions/unions.htm]

section's critique of Healy's opportunist politics and its relationship to his falsification of the dialectical method. When you, Comrade Steiner, left the movement in 1978, you were still in the thrall of Healy's "practice of cognition," which was, in essence, a variety of pragmatism, masquerading in a neo-Hegelian costume.

You missed out entirely on the important theoretical development that our movement was beginning to make. On November 7, 1978, a *Draft Resolution on the Perspectives and Tasks of the Workers League* was issued by the Political Committee. It included a section entitled "The historical continuity of Trotskyism as the basis of cadre training and the struggle against pragmatism." I will quote from the most important passage in this section:

> The orientation of the Workers League to the working class and its struggle to prepare the class for its historic role has not been a matter of a so-called "proletarian orientation" as conceived by Cannon. There can be no real turn to the working class outside of the conscious struggle to preserve the lines of historical continuity between the present struggles of the working class and the party as a unity of opposites and the whole content of historical experiences of the class and the development of Bolshevism. It is only from the standpoint of the struggle to base the whole work of the Party on the historical gains of the struggle against revisionism and the immense political and theoretical capital that is the heritage left behind by Trotsky to the Fourth International that the fight against pragmatism within the ranks of the Party and, therefore, in the working class itself can be seriously mounted. As soon as the struggle against pragmatism is detached from the fight to maintain the direct historical connec-

tions between the daily experiences through which the Trotskyist movement has passed, it degenerates into the most impotent forms of verbal jousting. Or, to put it even more accurately, it becomes simply another variety of pragmatism itself.

In place of rhetorical appeals for a "struggle against pragmatism," this analysis invested what had become an empty phrase under Healy and Slaughter with a politically concrete content. The document explained how Marxists, in contrast to the impressionistic and adaptive practice characteristic of pragmatists, seek to locate consciously the daily development of the class struggle and the activity of the party in the broad continuum of its own history and that of the international class struggle. Rather than simply react to events in pursuit of immediate or short-term practical gains, Marxists must identify the essential questions of political principle raised by these new developments, bring to bear in the analysis of the new political phenomenon the party's entire historically-accumulated theoretical capital, and give expression to the long-term interests of the working class as the international revolutionary force in capitalist society.

Four years later, in October 1982, the theoretical and political differences between the Workers League and the Workers Revolutionary Party in Britain emerged into the open. In an essay published in the *Bulletin* on October 19, 1982, the conceptions that had been originally developed in 1978 were expressed in more precise and pointed form:

> The history of Trotskyism cannot be comprehended as a series of disconnected episodes. Its theoretical development has been abstracted by its cadre from the continuous unfolding of the world capitalist crisis and the struggles of the international proletariat. Its un-

broken continuity of political analyses of all the fundamental experiences of the class struggle, *over an entire historical epoch*, constitutes the enormous richness of Trotskyism as the sole development of Marxism after the death of Lenin in 1924.

A leadership which does not strive collectively to assimilate the *whole* of this history cannot adequately fulfill its revolutionary responsibilities to the working class. Without a real knowledge of the historical development of the Trotskyist movement, references to dialectical materialism are not merely hollow; such empty references pave the way for real distortions of the dialectical method. The source of theory lies not in thought but in the objective world. Thus the development of Trotskyism proceeds from the fresh experiences of the class struggle which are posited on the entire historically-derived knowledge of our movement.

"Thus cognition rolls forward from content to content ... it raises to each next stage of determination the whole mass of the antecedent content, and by its dialectical progress not only loses nothing and leaves nothing behind, but carries with it all that it has acquired, enriching and concentrating itself upon itself..."

Quoting this passage from Hegel's *Science of Logic*, Lenin, in his "Philosophical Notebooks," wrote: "This extract is not at all bad as a kind of summing up of dialectics." (*Collected Works*, Volume 38, p. 230) Nor is this extract bad "as a kind of summing up of" the constant dialectical development of Trotskyist theory." [David North, *Leon Trotsky and the Development of Marxism*, (Detroit, 1985), pp. 18-19, emphasis in the original]

I will quote one further passage in which the relationship of dialectics to the struggle for revolutionary leadership in the working class was explained. It appeared as part of my obituary of Gerry Healy, following his death on December 14, 1989.

> In the long history of the Marxist movement, the dialectical method has proven itself an irreplaceable theoretical instrument of political prognosis, orientation and analysis. However, while the dialectical method, when utilized properly, facilitates the working out of farsighted analysis and effective tactical initiatives, it provides no once-and-for-all guarantees against political degeneration. Dialectical materialism is not some sort of ideological talisman which, once it has been acquired, bestows upon those who possess it protection against the relentless pressure of class forces. The touchstone of the dialectical method is a critical-revolutionary attitude to the existing production relations of society and the forms of appearance they spontaneously generate. It is a stern science and demands an unceasing struggle to establish, in program and practice, the independent attitude of the working class to every political question raised by the development of the class struggle. A revolutionary party remains "Marxist" only to the extent that it is fighting to overcome the pervasive political and ideological influence of the bourgeoisie and its agents over the working class. The Marxist approach to every significant event entails a reworking of the historical experiences of the international working class movement. Only by relentlessly confronting the fresh problems posed by the objective development of the class struggle with all the theoretical resources at its disposal can a Marxist party replenish and add to its theoretical capital. [*Gerry Healy and His Place in the History of the Fourth International* (Detroit, 1991), pp. 79-80]

These passages present the intellectual foundations of a theoretical-political project that has been pursued by the SEP with extraordinary consistency for more than a quarter-century (taking the perspectives resolution of 1978 as the beginning of this project). The International Committee of the Fourth International has sought to revive and develop the socialist consciousness of the working class based on a persistent and systematic reworking of the whole historical experience and lessons of the international class struggle in the 20th century, while at the same time seeking to base the practice of the working class on a scientific understanding of the significance and implications of contemporary socio-economic, political and cultural phenomena. The product of this theoretical work is recorded in the vast body of historical, political, economic and cultural analysis and commentary produced by the ICFI since the break with the Workers Revolutionary Party in 1985-86. The work of the 2005 summer school in Ann Arbor, followed by the 2006 meeting of the International Editorial Board, represented the highest achievement of this protracted and difficult project.

Both events could be succinctly described in theoretical terms as massive anti-pragmatic exercises. If the International Committee of the Fourth International had only the lectures and reports delivered at these two events to point to, that still would be sufficient to refute your provocative claim that dialectics is a "dead letter" in our movement and that the fight against pragmatism had been abandoned.[6]

---

6   The agenda of the school was as follows: Lecture I: The Russian Revolution and the unresolved historical problems of the 20th century (David North); Lecture II: Marxism versus revisionism on the eve of the twentieth century (David North); Lecture III: The origins of Bolshevism and *What Is To Be Done?* (David North); Lecture IV: Marxism, history and the science of perspective (David North); Lecture V: World War I: The breakdown of capitalism (Nick Beams); Lecture VI: Socialism in

6. What is objectivism?

If you were honest in your polemics and with yourselves, you would acknowledge that your attack on our alleged abandonment of dialectics and the fight against pragmatism is a subterfuge. The real issue is that you do not agree with the International Committee's insistence that the fight for socialism requires the development within the working class of both a profound knowledge of history – particularly that of the socialist movement itself – and as precise and concrete an understanding as possible (by means of ever-more exact conceptual approximations) of the objective movement of the world capitalist system in all its complex, contradictory and inter-connected forms. What you refer to falsely as "objectivism" is the Marxist striving to reflect accurately in subjective thought the law-governed movement of the objective world of which social man is a part, and to make this knowledge and understanding the basis of revolutionary practice. For all your talk about "dialectics" and the "fight against pragmatism," everything you write demonstrates indifference to the requirements of developing a working class movement whose practice is informed by Marxist theory.

Your usage of the word "objectivism" is incorrect, and reflects a basic disagreement with materialism. For Marxists, objectivism denotes a one-sided and abstract approach to the study of social phenomena that excludes all consideration of the activity of the conscious forces – that is, social classes and related political tendencies – that are critical elements in the objective

---

one country or permanent revolution (Bill Van Auken); Lecture VII: Marxism, art and the Soviet debate over "proletarian culture" (David Walsh); Lecture VIII: The 1920s: the road to depression and fascism (Nick Beams); Lecture IX: The rise of fascism in Germany and the collapse of the Communist International (Peter Schwarz).

process itself. As Lenin explained in his classic explanation of the difference between Marxism and objectivism:

> The objectivist speaks of the necessity of a given historical process; the materialist gives an exact picture of the given social-economic formation and of the antagonistic relations to which it gives rise. When demonstrating the necessity for a given series of facts, the objectivist always runs the risk of becoming an apologist for these facts: the materialist discloses the class contradictions and in so doing defines his standpoint. The objectivist speaks of "insurmountable historical tendencies"; the materialist speaks of the class which 'directs' the given economic system, giving rise to such and such forms of counteraction by other classes. Thus, on the one hand, the materialist is more consistent than the objectivist, and gives profounder and fuller effect to his objectivism. He does not limit himself to speaking of the necessity of a process, but ascertains exactly what class determines this necessity. In the present case, for example, the materialist would not content himself with stating the "insurmountable historical tendencies," but would point to the existence of certain classes, which determine the content of a given system and preclude the possibility of any solution except by the action of the producers themselves. On the other hand, materialism includes partisanship, so to speak, and enjoins the direct and open adoption of the standpoint of a definite social group in any assessment of events.[*Collected Works*, Volume 1 (Moscow, 1972), pp. 400-01, emphasis in the original]

Lenin does not use the term "objectivism" as an epithet directed against those who study the socio-economic processes that constitute the basis of revolutionary practice. Rather, he strives to impart a richer, more profoundly materialist content to the study of the objective world by demanding that it identify the class dynamics of any given social situation, and, on that basis, define as precisely as possible the political tasks of the revolutionary party. Lenin's vast theoretical output was characterized principally by his unrelenting determination to ground the perspective, program and activity of the Russian workers' movement in a precise and comprehensive understanding of objective reality. As you fling about the word "objectivism" one can only wonder how you would classify such crucial works of Lenin as *The Economic Content of Narodism*, *The Development of Capitalism in Russia*, and various massive studies, spanning several volumes, that he produced on the agrarian question in Russia (which Lenin considered to be an area in which he had developed a particular expertise).[7]

You tell us that "Marxist science is not a science in the conventional sense: its aim is not only to understand the world but also to transform it." But to what extent, Comrades Steiner and Brenner, is the revolutionary, i.e., historically progressive,

---

7   The immense importance that Lenin attributed to the cognition of objective social reality is clearly expressed in his *Materialism and Empirio-Criticism*:

   The fact that you live and conduct your business, beget children, produce products and exchange them, gives rise to an objectively necessary chain of development, which is independent of your *social* consciousness, and is never grasped by the latter completely. The highest task of humanity is to comprehend this objective logic of economic evolution (the evolution of social life) in its general and fundamental features, so that it may be possible to adapt *to it* one's social consciousness and the consciousness of the advanced classes of all capitalist countries in as definite, clear and critical fashion as possible. [*Collected Works*, Volume 14 (Moscow, 1977), p. 325, emphasis in the original.]

transformation of the world dependent upon a correct understanding of it? You need to think much more carefully about the answer you give to this question. Whether you call it "conventional" or "unconventional," Marxism can be considered a science only to the extent that the goal of its world-transforming practice – the ending of capitalist exploitation and the establishment of a socialist society – is based on a correct understanding of the laws of social development, rather than a mere desire for change, let alone a "will to power." In Marxism, the means by which revolutionists seek to transform the world is rooted in and inseparable from their understanding of the objective laws that govern the movement of society. This is a critical codicil of Marxist theory that cannot be violated without inviting political catastrophe and, I must add, moral shipwreck.

You write in the most haughtily abstract manner of the need for a struggle against pragmatism, but seem wholly unaware that it spawned numerous tendencies in the 20th century that sought to dissolve – through the extreme glorification of the transformative capacities of human practice – the essential ontological distinction, upon which dialectical materialism insists, between the objective world and the forms of its reflection in subjective consciousness. From the recognition that the world in which man lives is one acted upon and changed by human activity, certain pragmatic tendencies proclaimed it philosophically absurd to speak of an *objective* reality, existing independently of man, that places limits on man's activity. Thus, from the absence of an absolute separation between object and subject, they deduced the non-existence of even a relative separation. The subjective premises of James' pragmatism were developed in this extreme form by F.C.J. Schiller, Henri Bergson, Georges Sorel, and the Italians Giuseppe Prezzolini and Giovanni Pappini. The latter are particularly significant, inasmuch as the politically fascistic implications of the extreme forms of subjective voluntarism espoused in their pragmatism emerge most openly. Pappini wrote that pragmatism is

> A philosophy of action, a philosophy of doing, of rebuilding, transforming, creating! ... No more wild goose chasing down roads leading nowhere save into the snares and traps of visionary logicians. The True is the useful. To know is to do. Among the many uncertain truths, choose the one best calculated to raise the tone of life and promising the most lasting rewards. If something is not true but we wish it were true, we will make it true: by faith. [Quoted in *On Pragmatism*, by Cornelis De Waal (Wadsworth Philosophical Topics, 2005), p. 73, emphasis in the original]

Mussolini, who proclaimed himself an admirer of James' pragmatism, declared that "to fight for the establishment of that social order that *at the given moment* best corresponds to our *personal* ideal is one of the worthiest of human activities." [ibid. p. 74]

The issue here is not that pragmatists are inclined necessarily to become political reactionaries, let alone fascists. William James, as a matter of fact, was the most decent of human beings, and a leader of the anti-imperialist movement in the United States. But theoretical conceptions have a logic of their own; and the evolution of certain strains of pragmatic thought illustrates the dangerous implications of deprecating the Marxist effort to anchor political practice in a scientific study of the objective world. Pragmatic voluntarism can have disastrous results even in the context of radical left politics. A political initiative that is based on an impressionistic appraisal of the objective situation, which assumes that subjective determination can, under all circumstances, impart to the political situation a revolutionary potential that may not be present objectively, can leave the working class exposed to a devastating counter-attack.

This danger, I should stress, is not merely a theoretical possibility. The history of 20th century revolutionary movements is littered with the political and social wreckage created by voluntarist policies that ignored the objective logic of law-governed historical and socio-economic processes. Stalin's policies (i.e. collectivization, super-rapid industrialization) should provide sufficient proof of the disastrous consequences of policies formulated with insufficient knowledge of or indifference to the existing objective conditions and which exaggerate the transformative revolutionary potential of subjective will. Thus, the struggle for socialism requires that the tactics of the working class be based on a scientific understanding of the laws governing the world capitalist system, the international class struggle, and the forms of their reflection in mass consciousness. Herein lies the significance of perspective and the most exacting appraisal of the "objective situation," upon which the Trotskyist movement traditionally has placed such intense emphasis.[8]

---

8   One especially unpleasant expression of your indifference to political analysis is the manner in which you are willing to excuse even the grossest blunders of your utopian heroes. When comrade Steve Long pointed out to you, Comrade Steiner, that Jacoby (the author of your beloved *The End of Utopia*) is writing as a proponent of a liberal revival, you merely shrugged your shoulders and replied: "Does that mean that we as Marxists are therefore entitled to ignore everything he writes beyond page 8 where he announces his intentions of reviving a form of radical liberalism?" Or in response to comrade Long's reference to the unsavory political history of Herbert Marcuse and Theodor Adorno, you replied: "Yes, both Adorno and Marcuse were political opportunists who went along with the Moscow trials in the name of a 'united front' against fascism in the 1930s. Does that mean they had nothing relevant to say to us afterward?" Has it not occurred to you that the political swinishness

As I explained last summer, "Marxism, as a method of analysis and materialist world outlook, has uncovered laws that govern socio-economic and political processes. Knowledge of these laws discloses trends and tendencies upon which substantial historical 'predictions' can be based, and which allow the possibility of intervening consciously in a manner that may produce an outcome favorable to the working class."[9]

This is precisely what separates a Marxist practice from all forms of pragmatic activism, whether of a "left" adventurist or opportunist-adaptive character. As a matter of historical fact, the method of "objectivism" – which may lead depending on circumstances to one or the other political form – found its most developed expression in the Fourth International in the revisionist theories and politics of Pablo and his acolytes, Mandel and Hansen. Pabloite revisionism made a specialty of invoking demagogically, in an entirely abstract manner, the image of an all-powerful wave of revolutionary struggles that would – regardless of the political leaderships of those struggles and the masses' level of consciousness – sweep all obstacles before it and conquer power. As Cliff Slaughter explained so well (back in 1961 when he was still a Marxist):

---

of these individuals (and let us not forget to include Ernst Bloch, who greeted with rapture the murder of the Old Bolsheviks), had something to do with their utopianism? Why should confidence be placed in the utopian conceptions of individuals who were incapable of making a correct appraisal of objective reality, or even distinguishing truth from the noxious lies of the Stalinist regime? Would it be impolite to ask what method they employed when they considered political issues? Or perhaps their genius was of such a rarified and special character that it worked only in the future tense!

9   This is a passage from the fourth lecture, which included a substantial section devoted to the refutation of Sir Karl Popper's attack on Marxism. Your document contains not a single reference to this lecture and its attack on Popper's empiricism.

> The fundamental weakness of the SWP resolution is its substitution of 'objectivism,' i.e. a false objectivity, for the Marxist method ... From his analysis of imperialism as the final stage of capitalism, Lenin concluded that the conscious revolutionary role of the working class and its party was all-important. The protagonists of 'objectivism' conclude, however, that the strength of the 'objective factors' is so great that, *regardless* of the attainment of Marxist leadership of the proletariat in its struggle, the working-class revolution will be achieved, the power of the capitalists overthrown. [*Trotskyism Versus Revisionism*, Volume 3 (London, 1974), p. 161]

"Objectivism" as it is defined here by Cliff Slaughter in opposition to the Pabloites has absolutely nothing to do with your use of the term as an epithet directed against those who attempt to base revolutionary politics on a correct *Marxist* analysis of socio-economic phenomena. The Pabloites refused to make a concrete analysis of the world economy in the aftermath of World War II, let alone relate those changes to developments in the international class struggle. Indeed, Slaughter repeatedly challenged the SWP to justify its "objectivist" conclusions within the framework of "the general historical perspective of class relations." He stated that "The SWP must show in what way 'objective factors' in the world situation make it *unnecessary* in some cases to prepare and construct a revolutionary leadership." [ibid. p. 162] He also noted the connection between the "objectivism" of the Pabloites and their constant invocation of action, their demagogic references to "the 'impatience' of the masses who cannot delay the revolution until the construction of a Marxist leadership." [ibid.] Another characteristic of Pabloite objectivism was their glorification of the most elementary forms of working class mili-

tancy, which served as a justification for their own adaptation
to the existing bureaucratic leaders who invariably diverted the
mass movement away from its revolutionary political tasks.

And that is exactly where your deceitful denunciation of
our "objectivism" ends up. In the final analysis, your criticism
of our "objectivism" is a repudiation of the study and analysis
of socio-economic conditions and the class character of political tendencies that exercise influence on the working class.
Similarly, your denunciation of our "abstentionism" turns out
to be nothing more than a veiled attack on the party's assessment of the reactionary role of the trade unions. You state that
"It has been well over a decade since the party made the assessment that there was no longer any potential left for the
trade unions to play a progressive role, and yet in all that time
nothing has been done to propose any alternatives to the
working class. Nor has anything been done to work through
the implications of the degeneration of the unions with the
millions of workers still left within these organizations, since
apart from journalism any work inside the unions seems to
have long since been abandoned."

First of all, is our analysis of the trade unions correct or
incorrect? You fail to provide any analysis of the nature and
role of the AFL-CIO and other official trade union organizations. Do you believe that they retain the potential to play
what you call "a progressive role"? One may reasonably infer
from your attack that you still do. But why do you fail to state
this clearly, let alone explain on what you base your position?
Nor do you attempt a critical examination of the extensive
writings of the SEP and ICFI on the question of the trade
unions, in which the theoretical basis of our principled position has been elaborated. In a manner that reeks of the most
vulgar pragmatism, you complain that a worker who writes
into the *WSWS* asking for advice "is typically given a lecture
on the history of the labor bureaucracy but no indication

whatever on how to conduct the struggle he is involved in." But tell us, Comrades Steiner and Brenner, how is it possible for a worker to know how he should conduct a struggle in which he is immediately engaged without understanding the historical role of the trade unions? What are the implications of separating any given struggle in which workers are involved from the historical experience out of which it arose? Can a perspective for practical interventions in Russia be developed without educating workers in the history of Trotsky's struggle against Stalinism? Or in China? Or in Eastern Europe? Can a worker in the Middle East know "how to conduct the struggle he is involved in" without studying the historical role of bourgeois nationalism and the significance of Trotsky's theory of permanent revolution? How can the advanced sections of the Israeli working class find a way out of the blind alley of Jewish nationalism without understanding the origins and nature of Zionism? *To state the issue as precisely as possible, the "nature" of any given struggle can only be understood when placed in the necessary historical context.*

Your cheap gibe against the efforts of the *WSWS* to educate workers in history betrays, notwithstanding your rhetorical tributes to dialectics, an indifference to theory, which is derived from a painstaking review of the objective social experiences through which the working class has passed. As Trotsky explained so well, "To be guided by theory is to be guided by generalizations based on all preceding practical experiences of humanity in order to cope as successfully as possible with one or another practical problem of the present day. Thus, through theory we discover precisely the primacy of practice-as-a-whole over particular aspects of practice." ["Philosophical Tendencies of Bureaucratism," in *The Challenge of the Left Opposition 1928-29*, (New York, 1981) p. 396]

Tell us, Comrades Steiner and Brenner, what political generalizations have you drawn from the tragic experiences of the working class over the last 25 years? From the unending chain of defeats suffered by the American working class as a consequence of the criminal treachery of the bureaucratic organizations? In what way have you incorporated the experiences of the *international* working class into your understanding of the tasks confronting workers in the United States? What lessons have you drawn from the collapse of the Soviet Union and the Stalinist regimes in Eastern Europe, all of which were dissolved by the ruling bureaucracies? Or from the transformation of the "People's Republic" of China into the indispensable world center of low-wage capitalist industrial production? Or from the transformation of the British Labour Party into a vicious right-wing bourgeois party that has severed all connections with the working class? Or from the continued support of the Trades Union Congress for this party? We could continue with many more questions of this sort, but we can reasonably assume that no answer would be forthcoming. You have given no thought to the consequences, for both political perspectives and practice, of the collapse of all the traditional political and trade union organizations of the working class during the past quarter-century.

7. The New York City transit strike

While you prefer to conduct your polemical battles in the realm of abstract generalities, on the one occasion when you descend to the world of actual events, the political content of your denunciation of our "objectivism" becomes clear. You are opposed to the struggle waged by the Socialist Equality Party and the *WSWS* against the trade union bureaucracy. Your lengthy attack on the party's role in the New York City transit strike aims to discredit our effort to arm transit workers with a political perspective. However, before answering your attack in detail, it is worth noting that the transit strike is the only event to which you actually refer in your entire document. Could you not at least have referred to one event that occurred outside the city in which you live? Why not an examination of the party's campaign against the war in Iraq? Or the intervention of the ICFI in the crisis in France? Or the struggle conducted by our comrades in Sri Lanka against the government's efforts to renew the war against the Tamils? None of this interests you. Given the fact that no other events are referred to – not even the war in Iraq – the attention that you lavish on the transit strike is entirely out of balance. At the very least, it expresses a provincial outlook.

Your portrayal of the SEP's intervention as a mixture of confusion and inaction reeks of factionally-motivated dishonesty. Your review of events lacks all concreteness. You refer to "the three-day strike in December [2005]," but do not even specify the actual dates during which it took place. This is not a minor omission. No one who depended on your account would be able to relate objective developments to the intervention of the SEP. You write that "Though there was a long buildup to this strike and though this was a union where the party had a long history, there were no demands raised until the day before the strike began." Along with the absence of a specific time frame, your critique does not quote a single sentence from anything written by the SEP on the transit strike. No one who read your document would have any way of forming a precise conception of the scale of the party's intervention or the program for which it fought.

As your attack on the party's intervention in the transit strike is intended to demonstrate the "objectivism" and "abstentionism" of the party, it is necessary to reply in considerable detail. The strike began on Tuesday, December 20, and ended on Thursday, December 22. Your document gives readers the impression that the SEP was taken unawares by devel-

opments, and only managed to issue a statement on the very
eve of the strike.

Let us now reconstruct the actual response of the party to
the transit struggle.

On December 10, 2005, ten days before the strike began,
the *WSWS* published a lengthy statement, written by Alan
Whyte, which analyzed the central issues raised in the conflict
between Transport Workers Union Local 100 and the New
York Metropolitan Transportation Authority (MTA). After
a careful factual review of the contractual dispute, Whyte
wrote:

> It has been 25 years since the last transit strike, when
> workers shut down the system for 11 days. In that
> quarter of a century, workers in New York City and
> across the US have seen their incomes steadily eroding
> along with the loss of millions of decent-paying jobs,
> the destruction of social benefits and an assault on ba-
> sic democratic rights. These attacks have created the
> conditions for the staggering growth of social inequal-
> ity as vast wealth has been transferred into the bank
> accounts of the top 1 percent.
>
> The unions have proven incapable of combating these
> attacks. Rather, under the control of an opportunist
> bureaucracy subservient to the Democratic Party and
> the profit system, they have collaborated in the imposi-
> tion of an unending series of concessions.
>
> There is no question that a transit workers' strike,
> demonstrating the power of the working class to defy
> the dictates of Wall Street, would win powerful sup-
> port in New York City and across the country. A seri-
> ous struggle to defend living standards and reverse the
> attacks of the past 25 years, however, means more than
> militant strike action.

It above all requires a political struggle to mobilize working people as a whole in opposition to the profit system. This means a break with the Democratic Party and the building of an independent political party of the working class fighting to reorganize society to meet human needs, rather than the accumulation of wealth by a financial elite.

Only such a party will fight to provide full funding for mass transit by repudiating the bond debts and bringing the immense resources of the finance houses and banks that have profited off these debts under public ownership.

This statement was published as a leaflet and circulated among transit workers. Thus, 10 days before the strike actually began (after a postponement by the TWU leadership), the *WSWS* issued a clear political-programmatic statement. Two days later, on December 12, the *WSWS* published another article by Whyte reporting the authorization vote for a strike that was originally set for midnight, December 16. The article warned of the duplicity of the union officials, and noted that the presence of the political charlatan Jesse Jackson at the strike-vote rally was a clear sign that the TWU leadership was committed to its politically-bankrupt alliance with the Democratic Party.

On December 16, the *WSWS* published an analysis by Bill Van Auken, entitled "The political issues confronting New York City transit workers." It alerted transit workers to Mayor Bloomberg's preparations for a massive legal assault against the union. It stressed that the union could not conduct a successful strike without fighting to mobilize the broadest sections of the working class. But the statement warned that "There is no indication that the leadership of TWU Local 100 is preparing to mount such a struggle. The union bureaucracy, headed by

Local 100 President Roger Toussaint, appeals strictly to the lowest common denominator of trade union militancy. At the same time, it is promoting Democratic politicians as friends of workers."

On December 17, Van Auken reported on the TWU's decision to delay a full-scale walkout and call selective strikes.

On December 19, a statement entitled "New York City transit workers on brink of class confrontation," by Peter Daniels, was posted on the *WSWS* (and printed and circulated as a leaflet). It reviewed the lessons of the major experiences through which the American working class had passed since the betrayal of the New York transit strike in April 1980 and the destruction of PATCO in 1981. The statement stressed the need for a political strategy: "The truth about this struggle must be stated from the outset. Either the transit workers' struggle enlists the active support of other sections of workers in a political counteroffensive against all the attacks on jobs and public services, or it will be isolated and defeated." It also warned that "Any reliance upon Toussaint to conduct this struggle would be a grievous mistake. The Local 100 president combines the occasional demagogic threat with support for the big business Democratic Party and opposition to the independent struggle of the working class." The statement called upon workers to "organize independent strike committees to bring the message of unity and struggle to all sections of working people – to other trade unionists, to the unorganized and unemployed, the immigrants, the students, youth, professionals and small business."

Your principal criticism of this statement, from which you fail to quote a single sentence, is that the *WSWS* "gave no indication of how these committees should be set up, how they should function and above all what they should fight for." No, we did not attempt to write a manual on how to form strike committees. To the extent that workers understood the need for an alternative to the TWU Local 100 leadership and its policies, they would be more than capable of working out the details of creating and running rank-and-file strike committees. But we most certainly did explain what such committees should fight for: the statement outlined the political strategy upon which the fate of the strike depended. One can only assume from this criticism that you did not agree with the emphasis placed by the *WSWS* on the need for transit workers to conduct a political fight – which was the only way that support could be rallied among masses of New York workers, for whom the strike created additional daily hardships.

On December 21, the *WSWS* posted a new statement (also printed and mass distributed throughout the city): "The New York transit strike: A new stage in the class struggle." It examined the implications of the struggle within the context of the social polarization within the United States, and exposed the financial interests underlying the brutal legal assault directed by Mayor Bloomberg against the transit workers. The statement attacked the insidious role played by the TWU International leadership, which had denounced the strike as illegal and called for an immediate return to work. It concluded with a summation of the political issues:

> More starkly than any event in the past twenty years, the present strike by New York City transit workers poses before the entire working class the need to develop a new leadership and a new political strategy to carry forward their struggle, founded on a program that upholds the interests and needs of working people against the profit drive of the financial elite. …
>
> If this strike is to be successful, transit workers must be guided by a perspective that rejects the social, economic and political assumptions of the financial oligarchy and its political parties. The unending demands for

a reduction in the living standards of workers clearly demonstrate that their interests are incompatible with the requirements of the capitalist profit system.

In addition to this statement, the *WSWS* posted on December 21 numerous interviews with striking workers.

On December 22, the *WSWS* posted another major statement (also printed and mass distributed) entitled "New York transit workers confront escalating attacks." It reviewed the political strategy of Mayor Bloomberg and Governor Pataki, and the reasons for the vicious response to the strike. The statement explained why the ruling elite viewed the strike as a major challenge that had to be defeated. The *WSWS* contrasted the solidarity within the ruling class to the efforts of the labor bureaucracy to isolate and sabotage the strike. It warned that a major betrayal was being prepared, and repeated its call for workers to "organize their own independent strike committees and turn out to the broadest sections of the working class to mobilize support."

The *WSWS* also published more interviews with striking workers.

On December 23, the *WSWS* published a statement that offered a "preliminary assessment" of the sudden end of the strike. It offered a blunt and sober assessment of the outcome of the strike, which was isolated by the union bureaucracy. The *WSWS* stated that Toussaint "conducted the strike as a pure-and-simple trade union struggle under conditions in which the transit workers were confronting the full power of the state mobilized through the Taylor Law and the courts." Drawing the broader lessons of this experience, the *WSWS* stressed that the strike had refuted all those who claimed that the working class had disappeared as a social force. In shutting down the entire transit system, the working class had demonstrated its immense social weight and combativity. However, the struggle "also exposed the existing trade unions as hopelessly inadequate instruments of social struggle. To the extent that these organizations are not actively engaged in the suppression of the working class – as in the case of the TWU International and the AFL-CIO as a whole – their lack of an alternative political, social and economic perspective and program leaves them defenseless against the attacks of the state. Dominated by a politically reactionary bureaucracy allied with the Democratic Party, they are inevitably transformed into a means of imposing the demands of the ruling elite on the working class." The *WSWS* called for "a new socialist movement capable of uniting the working class on the basis of an uncompromising anti-capitalist line."

On December 24, another major statement (also printed and mass distributed) was published by the *WSWS*, providing further details on the way the unions sabotaged the Local 100 strike.

Your attack on the intervention of the party in the transit strike is without substance. You take it for granted that your readers will not have access to the written record. However, if we review the response of the *WSWS* to the struggle of the transit workers, we find that during the two week period between December 10 and December 24, it published six major policy statements and another eight articles that were either extensive news reports, interviews with transit workers, or commentary on various social issues related to the class divide in New York City. Of these 14 items, eight were printed and mass distributed.[10] This is the record that supposedly epitomizes the "abstentionism" of the SEP! The response to the transit strike demonstrated the critical role played by the *WSWS* in the fight to develop a new political strategy in the

---

10 During this period, the *WSWS* maintained its rigorous coverage of other major national and international events.

struggles of the working class. It should also be noted that
during this entire period, the union itself did not publish or
distribute a single statement for mass distribution, let alone
provide daily analysis of the ongoing struggle. The *WSWS*
was not able single-handedly to overcome the sabotage of
the bureaucracy. However, it contributed significantly toward
raising the class consciousness of the workers, and laying the
foundations for future victories.

I will not be so impolite as to ask for a detailed account of
Comrade Steiner's practical contributions to the struggle, but
it is rather noticeable that you fail to tell us what your activities consisted of during the strike. What, if anything, did you
do? What did you write? Did you draft a statement, perhaps
with the title "The Transit Strike and Utopia"? Perhaps difficulties of one sort or another compelled you to forgo direct
involvement in the strike. If so, there is no need to offer apolo-
gies. However, it is disappointing that you have not taken the
opportunity afforded by your critique to explain, at least theoretically, how utopianism would have looked in action. We are
entitled to conclude that your utopian schemes are largely intended for discussions within petty-bourgeois radical circles.
When it comes to the workers, you have nothing for them
except the thin gruel of trade unionism.

8. The WSWS and "political exposures"

Now let us return to your analysis of my conception of
the struggle for socialist consciousness. Referring to (but not
quoting from) my lecture on *What Is To Be Done?*, you state
that "North tries to shoehorn Lenin into providing a justification for this abstentionism by highlighting the phrase 'political exposures' by which Lenin contrasted his approach to
developing class consciousness to the Economists' focus on

bread-and-butter issues. North jumps on this phrase because it seems to sanction the journalistic existence of the *WSWS*, but it is nonsense to suppose that Lenin saw this phrase as some sort of all-purpose recipe for dealing with an issue as complex as the development of class consciousness."

The worst sort of polemics, Comrades Steiner and Brenner, is that which either assumes or appeals to the ignorance of readers. And that is precisely the method you employ. As I have already noted, you never quote accurately and in context from any of my reports. Your aim is not to educate but to mislead and deceive. In your attack on my analysis of *What Is To Be Done?*, you quote neither my lecture nor any part of the text of Lenin's seminal work to which I referred. "Political Exposures" is not a phrase that I "highlighted" (i.e., exaggerated) in order to provide a false authority for the work of the *WSWS*. These words actually appear as part of the title of the third section ("Political Exposures and Training in Revolutionary Activity") of Chapter II, "The Spontaneity of the Masses and the Consciousness of Social Democrats." As employed by Lenin, "Political Exposures" is not a mere phrase, but rather a central concept in his theory of socialist consciousness. This concept developed over several years in the course of the struggle against Economism, which was the specific form taken by Bernsteinite revisionism in Russia. The latter tendency sought to replace the revolutionary Social Democratic concentration on the political education of the working class, to which Plekhanov and Lenin attributed primary and overriding importance, with agitation over economic issues along conventional militant trade unionist lines. Lenin wrote in the third section of Chapter II:

> A basic condition for the necessary expansion of
> political agitation is the organization of *comprehen-*

sive political exposure. In no way except by means of such exposures can the masses be trained in political consciousness and revolutionary activity. Hence, activity of this kind is one of the most important functions of international Social-Democracy as a whole, for even political freedom does not in any way eliminate exposures; it merely shifts somewhat their sphere of direction.[*Collected Works*, Volume 5 (Moscow, 1961), p. 412, emphasis in the original]

Lenin continued:

Working-class consciousness cannot be genuine political consciousness unless the workers are trained to respond to *all* cases of tyranny, oppression, violence, and abuse, no matter what class is affected – unless they are trained, moreover, to respond from a Social-Democratic point of view and no other. The consciousness of the working masses cannot be genuine class-consciousness unless the workers learn, from concrete, and above all from topical, political facts and events to observe every other social class in all the manifestations of its intellectual, ethical, and political life; unless they learn to apply in practice the materialist analysis and the materialist estimate of all aspects of the life and activity of all classes, strata, and groups of the population. [ibid. emphasis in the original]

At the conclusion of the same paragraph, Lenin states that "These comprehensive political exposures are an essential and *fundamental* condition for training the masses in revolutionary activity." [ibid. p. 413, emphasis in the original]

Attempting to disparage the work of the ICFI, you refer contemptuously to "the journalistic existence of the *WSWS*," and even equate political exposures with mere "journalism."[11] This is nothing more than an appeal to political backwardness and anti-intellectualism. You are attacking the International Committee for creating an organ through which it presents its analysis and program to a world audience of socialist and politically progressive workers, intellectuals and young people. Only those who oppose the struggle for Marxism and socialist ideas would disparage such essential activity. Would you prefer that the work of political analysis be left to the reactionary bourgeois press, or to the left-liberal advisers of the Democratic Party in such publications as *Salon* and *The Nation* (which has recently devoted considerable resources to the development of its web site), or to the myriad perpetually disoriented petty-bourgeois radical groups?

At any rate, since when have Marxists considered it inappropriate to concentrate their energies on the publication of a theoretical and political organ? As you well know, the creation of a political newspaper, *Iskra*, represented a milestone in the Russian socialist movement. This was a task to which Lenin had devoted years of his early political life. As he wrote in 1901, in his article *Where to Begin*:

> In our opinion, the starting-point of our activities, the first step toward creating the desired organization, or, let us say, the main thread which, if followed, would enable us steadily to develop, deepen, and extend that

---

11 One is entitled to ask when journalism, the occupation of so many revolutionary Marxists, became a term of abuse? What little money Marx earned came from his work as a journalist. Prior to 1917, Trotsky listed "journalist" as his profession. Countless other Marxists practiced this profession. One might say, following Wilde, that it is neither moral nor immoral to practice journalism. The issue is whether one does it well or badly, as a conscientious observer and analyst, or as a propagandist and apologist for the interests of the ruling elite.

organization, should be the founding of an All-Russian political newspaper. A newspaper is what we most of all need; without it we cannot conduct that systematic, all-round propaganda and agitation, consistent in principle, which is the chief and permanent task of Social-Democracy in general and, in particular, the pressing task of the moment, when interests in politics and in questions of socialism has been aroused among the broadest strata of the population. ... Without a political organ, a political movement deserving of the name is inconceivable in the Europe of today. Without such a newspaper, we cannot possibly fulfill our task – that of concentrating all the elements of political discontent and protest, of vitalizing thereby the revolutionary movement of the proletariat. We have taken the first step, we have aroused in the working class a passion for "economic," factory exposures; we must now take the next step, that of arousing in every section of the population that is at all politically conscious a passion for *political* exposure. [ibid. p. 20-21, emphasis in the original]

Sensing that your dismissal of "political exposures" is extremely vulnerable to theoretical rebuttal, you suddenly shift gears and assert that "it is no disservice to Lenin to note that times have changed since 1902: today's petty-bourgeois radicals, unlike their Economist predecessors, are far removed not only from bread-and-butter issues but from anything to do with the working class."

Here you manage to combine an empty cliché, a political non-sequitur, and a clearly false statement in just one sentence. You tell us that "times have changed." Yes, we all know that we live in 2006, not 1902. But what is it in the present situation that has diminished the relevance of the principled and theoretically-grounded emphasis that Lenin placed on the development of political consciousness in the working class? The concept of political exposures arose out of an analysis of the problem, rooted in the very nature of capitalist society, of developing the class consciousness of the proletariat. The relevance of that analysis could be diminished only if there has occurred such basic structural changes in the capitalist mode of production and the general organization of bourgeois society that the development of socialist class consciousness no longer required the additional impulse of Marxist-inspired political exposures. But if this were the case, then we would be compelled to reconsider the relevance of Lenin's more general claim that socialist consciousness cannot develop spontaneously, that it must be introduced into the working class from the outside.

You assert that a critical difference between present conditions and those of 1902, which therefore lessens the importance of political exposures, is that petty-bourgeois radicals are completely different from the old Economists in that they "are far removed not only from bread-and-butter issues but from anything at all to do with the working class."

First of all, the relevance of Lenin's theory of consciousness depends not on what forms of activity petty-bourgeois radicals may or may not be engaged in, but upon the objective structure and social relations of capitalist society. Second, your claim is absolutely false from a factual standpoint. The present-day bureaucracy of the trade unions is *saturated* with middle-class refugees from the radical political organizations of the 1960s, 1970s and 1980s. The president of the SEIU, Andrew Stern, is only one of scores of ex-radicals who have made careers in the upper councils of the labor bureaucracy. The New Directions movement that controls TWU Local 100 is the creation of various radical tendencies. The petty-bourgeois radical Solidarity tendency is deeply integrated into the bureaucracy of various unions. And we might point out that none other than Nancy Fields Wohlforth, whom I am sure you remember, has recently been elected to the International Executive Board of the AFL-CIO.[12] So much for the claim that petty-bourgeois radicals have nothing "at all to do with the working class." The exact opposite is the case: they have become the most fanatical converts to trade union opportunism in its most reactionary forms. Their activities are directed ruthlessly against the development of socialist political activity in the working class.

Your next argument against the *WSWS* is an absurdity. You tell us that political exposures are to be found "on a plethora of radical websites on the internet and in the increasingly popular medium of documentary filmmaking. Michael Moore has become famous producing 'political exposures,' but this is still very far from class consciousness, and the gap is painfully evident in the way a film like *Fahrenheit 9/11* was used to enlist support for the Democrats."

Do you expect this to be taken as a serious argument against the work of the *WSWS*? What conclusion is to be drawn from your dubious syllogism: 1) The *WSWS* produces political exposures; 2) Michael Moore produces political exposures; therefore 3) the politics of the *WSWS* and the politics of Michael Moore are the same? Or, perhaps, 1) Petty-bourgeois radicals produce political exposures; 2) *WSWS* writers produce political exposures; therefore 3) *WSWS* writers are petty-bourgeois radicals?

---

12 Her evolution entirely substantiates the assessment that we jointly made of Fields and her former husband, Tim Wohlforth, in the pamphlet that you, Comrade Steiner, and I co-authored more than 30 years ago, *The Fourth International and the Renegade Wohlforth*. I would strongly encourage you to re-read this work.

You conclude this section of your document with the following astonishing statement, "If Lenin were alive today, he'd be far more likely to say that while 'political exposures' are all well and good, the crying need is for Marxists to do what they can to fill the immense vacuum of leadership in struggles like those of the transit workers." Lenin as a trade union activist! If that is true, then it is just as possible that Marx, were he alive today, might be running the arbitrage department at the Deutsche Bank. And Engels, perhaps, would be the CEO of Daimler Benz. But then these re-incarnations would not be Marx, Engels and Lenin.

9. The 2004 Election

In your next paragraph, you assert that I was unable, on account of my alleged objectivist and mechanical conception of consciousness, to explain the results of the 2004 elections, and that I considered the result of the election "inexplicable." On this one occasion, you actually quote one complete sentence – from a lecture that I gave in November 2004 on the results of the recently completed election, in which I referred to the majority pro-Bush vote in the most impoverished states: "To claim that its voters backed the Republicans because of 'values' that they hold far dearer than their own material interests is to substitute mysticism for scientific socio-political analysis." You end the quote there (without providing a page reference), and proclaim: "But this leaves us completely at a loss to understand what happened in the election, since clearly values of some kind played a role in that."

If the sentence that you cited were all that I said, it would have been inadequate as an explanation of why Bush swept the most impoverished states. But, as a matter of fact, it was actually the beginning of an extended analysis that you leave out. I went on to say (immediately after that sentence) the following:

> Abstract references to "values," whose precise meaning is clear to no one, do little to explain why workers have come under the influence of the Republican Party and its retinue of religious hucksters and moralizing conmen. A more convincing explanation is that the virtual collapse of the old labor movement in states that were once bastions of militant trade unionism has left millions of workers without any means of confronting social problems and defending their interests as a class. Let us consider the social experience of just one section of the American working class. For much of the twentieth century, the struggles of coal miners, organized inside the UMWA, raged across West Virginia and Kentucky, as well as significant sections of Virginia, Tennessee, Arkansas, Ohio and even Indiana. The coal miners were arguably the most class conscious section of the American working class. They fought "with fine impartiality"—as John L. Lewis might have said— mighty coal corporations and defied the White House on innumerable occasions. But during the 1980s the miners suffered a series of devastating defeats, for which the treachery of the union bureaucracy was principally responsible, that reduced the UMWA to a hollow and insignificant shell. Thousands of coal mining jobs were wiped out.
>
> Without jobs, cut off from the deep-rooted social relations that sustained class consciousness over generations of struggle, alienated from a union that had deserted them, the militant workers of yesterday became susceptible to well-practiced pitchmen of the Evangelical Industry, always on the look-out for new

customers. For the children of such workers, who have grown up entirely outside the milieu of an organized labor movement and with little or no awareness of the traditions of class struggle, the obstacles to the development of class consciousness are considerable. From what source will they acquire the information and insights that facilitate the development of a critical attitude toward contemporary society, let alone a sense that a better and more humane society—*in this world and in their lifetime*—is possible? Certainly not from the existing political parties or from the cesspool of the mass media.

This does not mean that the average American worker buys into the propaganda to which he or she is subjected relentlessly by the mass media and the Republican political machine. Not by a long shot. They see enough of life to know that things are not as they should be. When a worker speaks of "values," it has a very different meaning for him than it does for Enron's Kenneth Lay or for George Bush.

A number of reports have emerged that already call into question the significance of the 'values' issue in the 2004 Election. It now appears that the polling data upon which the initial post-election claims were made were either misleading or misinterpreted. This, I am sure, is the case. But the really important point that must be made is that the 'values' issue has arisen in a political vacuum created by the absence of any articulation by either party of the genuine social, economic and political interests of the broad mass of working Americans. The Democrats, the Republicans and the mass media form different parts of one massive chorus that sings rapturous hymns to the glories of American capitalism.

This is not a temporary weakness that can be overcome through a reshuffling of personnel or the recruitment of better candidates. It is a product of the evolution of American capitalism, the extraordinary concentration of wealth in relatively few hands, the extreme levels of social inequality, the rapid decline of the traditional 'middle class' strata that once served as arbitrators in the class struggle between capitalists and workers and which formed a substantial constituency for social reformism, and, finally, the disappearance within the ruling elite itself of any substantial bloc seriously committed to the maintenance of traditional bourgeois democratic forms of rule." [*The Crisis of American Democracy: The Presidential Elections of 2000 and 2004* (Detroit, 2004), pp. 104-05, emphasis in the original]

It is quite clear that I did not at all consider the outcome of the election "inexplicable." You simply chose not to quote my explanation. But the falsification does not end there. You then assert that I, as a "mechanical materialist," assume that "consciousness will accurately comprehend the reality that shaped it, i.e., that objective conditions translate themselves directly into a *correct* consciousness of those conditions." Such a conception is, indeed, incorrect. However, as you well know, I never said any such thing. As a matter of fact, I devoted a substantial portion of the third lecture that I delivered last summer to an explanation of why the consciousness that arises spontaneously within the working class is not socialist consciousness. As a consequence of your unscrupulous approach to polemics, in which you are prepared to attribute to your political opponents positions that are the opposite of what they believe and have actually said, I am again obligated to provide a lengthy extract from my lecture:

When people go to work, to what extent are they aware of the vast network of global economic interconnections of which their own job is a minute element? One can reasonably assume that even the most intelligent worker would have only the vaguest sense of the relationship of his job, or his company, to the immensely complex processes of modern transnational production and exchange of goods and services. Nor is the individual worker in a position to penetrate the mysteries of international capitalist finance, the role of global hedge funds, and the secret and often impenetrable ways (even to experts in the field) that tens of billions of dollars in financial assets are moved across international borders every day. The realities of modern capitalist production, trade and finance are so complex that corporate and political leaders are dependent upon the analyses and advice of major academic institutions, which, more often than not, are divided among themselves as to the meaning of data at their disposal.

But the problem of class consciousness goes beyond the obvious difficulty of assimilating and mastering the complex phenomena of modern economic life. At a more basic and essential level, the precise nature of the social relationship between an individual worker and his employer, let alone between the entire working class and the bourgeoisie, is not and cannot be grasped at the level of sense perception and immediate experience.

Even a worker who is convinced that he or she is being exploited cannot, on the basis of his or her own bitter personal experience, perceive the underlying socio-economic mechanism of that exploitation. Moreover, the concept of exploitation is not one that is easily understood, let alone derived directly from the instinctive sense that one is not being paid enough. The worker who fills out an application form upon applying for a job does not perceive that she is offering to sell her labor power, or that the unique quality of that labor power is its capacity to produce a sum of value greater than the price (the wage) at which it has been purchased; and that profit is derived from this differential between the cost of labor power and the value that it creates.

Nor is a worker aware that when he purchases a commodity for a definite sum of money, the essence of that exchange is a relation not between things (a coat or some other commodity for a definite amount of money) but between people. Indeed, he does not understand the nature of money, how it emerged historically as the expression of the value form, and how it serves to mask, in a society in which the production and exchange of commodities have been universalized, the underlying social relations of capitalist society.

What I have just been speaking about might serve as a general introduction to what might be considered the theoretical-epistemological foundation of Marx's most important work, *Capital*. In the concluding section of the critical chapter one of volume one, Marx introduces his theory of commodity fetishism, which explains the objective source of the mystification of social relations within capitalist society—that is, the reason why in this particular economic system social relations between people necessarily appear as relations between things. It is not, and cannot be apparent to workers, on the basis of sense perception and immediate experience, that any given commodity's value is the crystallized expression of the sum of human labor expended in its production. The discovery of the objective essence of the value form represented a historical milestone in scientific thought. Without this discovery, neither the objective socio-economic foundations of the class struggle nor their revolutionary implications could have been understood.

However the worker may dislike the social consequences of the system in which he lives, he is not in a position to grasp, on the basis of immediate experience, either its origins, its internal contradictions or the historically-limited character of its existence. The understanding of the contradictions of the capitalist mode of production, of the exploitative relationship between capital and wage-labor, of the inevitability of class struggle and its revolutionary consequences, arose on the basis of real scientific work, with which the name of Marx will be forever linked. The knowledge obtained through this science, and the method of analysis involved in the achievement and extension of this knowledge, must be introduced into the working class. That is the task of the revolutionary party.

These passages, quoted directly from last summer's lectures, advance a position that is the absolute opposite of that which you attribute to me.

10. Marxism and the Enlightenment

A principled approach to polemics requires that the arguments of an opponent be presented accurately. The fact that you are unable to do this, that you feel compelled to mislead and misrepresent – in effect, to lie – has, itself, serious and disturbing political implications. As Trotsky pointed out, the lie serves an essential function in political life: it is employed to conceal social interests and to cover over weaknesses and contradictions in a political position. In your case, the dishonest methods flow from your efforts to pose publicly as a Marxist while having rejected – and not all that unconsciously – the theoretical and political foundations of Marxism. Your differences with the International Committee are not over isolated programmatic points, but rather over the most fundamental questions of philosophical world outlook upon which the struggle for socialism is based.

Before you rise from your seat to protest this "slur" on your revolutionary honor, permit me to point out that your document includes passages which are totally alien to the world-historical outlook of Marxism. A particularly noteworthy example is your statement that my "critique of postmodernism is used to sanction an uncritical defense of the Enlightenment."

The passage in my first lecture to which you are referring, but do not quote, appears in a section entitled "Historical consciousness versus postmodernism." I said the following:

> The conception of history that we uphold, which assigns to the knowledge and theoretical assimilation of historical experience such a critical and decisive role in the struggle for human liberation, is irreconcilably hostile to all prevailing trends of bourgeois thought. The political, economic and social decay of bourgeois society is mirrored, if not spearheaded, by its intellectual degradation. In a period of political reaction, Trotsky once noted, ignorance bares its teeth.
>
> The specific and peculiar form of ignorance championed today by the most skilled and cynical academic representatives of bourgeois thought, the postmodernists, is *ignorance of and contempt for history*. The postmodernists' extreme rejection of the validity of history and the central role assigned to it by all genuine progressive trends of social thought is inextricably linked with another essential element of their theoretical

conceptions—the denial and explicit repudiation of objective truth as a significant, let alone central, goal of philosophical inquiry.

What, then, is postmodernism? Permit me to quote, as an explanation, a passage written by a prominent academic defender of this tendency, Professor Keith Jenkins:

"Today we live within the general condition of *postmodernity*. We do not have a choice about this. For postmodernity is not an 'ideology' or a position we can choose to subscribe to or not; postmodernity is precisely our condition: it is our fate. And this condition has arguably been caused by the general failure—a general failure which can now be picked out very clearly as the dust settles over the twentieth century—of that experiment in social living that we call modernity. It is a general failure, as measured in its own terms, of the attempt, from around the eighteenth century in Europe, to bring about through the application of reason, science and technology, a level of personal and social wellbeing within social formations, which, legislating for an increasingly generous emancipation of their citizens/subjects, we might characterize by saying that they were trying, at best, to become 'human rights communities.'

"... [T]here are not now—nor have there ever been—any 'real' foundations of the kind alleged to underpin the experiment of the modern."

Permit me, if I may use the language of the postmodernists, to "deconstruct" this passage. For more than two hundred years, stretching back into the eighteenth century, there were people, inspired by the science and philosophy of the Enlightenment, who believed in progress, in the possibility of human perfectibility, and who sought the revolutionary transformation of society on the basis of what they believed to be a scientific insight into the objective laws of history.

Such people believed in History (with a capital H) as a law-governed process, determined by socio-economic forces existing independently of the subjective consciousness of individuals, but which men could discover, understand and act upon in the interests of human progress.

But all such conceptions, declare the postmodernists, have been shown to be naïve illusions. We now know better: there is no History (with a capital H). There is not even history (with a small h), understood merely as an objective process. There are merely subjective "narratives," or "discourses," with shifting vocabularies employed to achieve one or another subjectively-determined useful purpose, whatever that purpose might be.

From this standpoint, the very idea of deriving "lessons" from "history'" is an illegitimate project. There is really nothing to be studied and nothing to be learned. As Jenkins insists, "[W]e now just have to understand that we live amidst social formations which have no legitimizing ontological or epistemological or ethical grounds for our beliefs beyond the status of an ultimately self-referencing (rhetorical) conversation... Consequently, we recognize today that there never has been, and there never will be, any such thing as a past which is expressive of some sort of essence."

Translated into comprehensible English, what Jenkins is saying is that 1) the functioning of human societies, either past or present, cannot be understood in terms of objective laws that can be or are waiting to be discovered; and 2) there is no objective foundation underlying what people may think, say, or do about the society in which they live. People who call themselves historians may advance one or another interpretation of the past, but replacement of one interpretation with another does not express an advance toward something objectively truer than what was previously written—for there is no objective truth to get closer to. It is merely the replacement of one way of talking about the past with another way of talking about the past—for reasons suited to the subjectively-perceived uses of the historian.

The proponents of this outlook assert the demise of modernity, but refuse to examine the whole complex of historical and political judgments upon which their conclusions are premised. They do, of course, hold political positions which both underlie and find expression in their theoretical views. Professor Hayden White, one of the leading exponents of postmodernism, has stated explicitly, "Now I am against revolutions, whether launched from 'above' or 'below' in the social hierarchy and whether directed by leaders who profess to possess a science of society and history or be celebrators of political 'spontaneity.'"

The legitimacy of a given philosophical conception is not automatically refuted by the politics of the individual by whom it is advanced. But the anti-Marxist and anti-socialist trajectory of postmodernism is so evident that it is virtually impossible to disentangle its theoretical conceptions from its political perspective.

You proceed to attack this analysis, writing in response:

Anyone defending the Enlightenment heritage of reason is progressive and anyone against is reactionary. But this crude dichotomy obscures the important truth that in the battle over reason Marxism has to fight on *two* fronts – against irrationalism (whether in the form of religious mysticism or the Nihilism of the Nietzsche-Heidegger line and its postmodern derivatives) but also against the much more pervasive "reason" of bourgeois society that rationalizes class domination (notably in the form of pragmatism and empiricism). In the latter sense Marxism represents a dialectical negation of the Enlightenment: Marx stripped away the "reason" of the Enlightenment philosophes and uncovered the rationalizations of a new form of class oppression.

This is a complete muddle. First of all, your use of the pronoun "anyone" is sufficiently obscure to prevent the reader from clearly identifying the tendencies to which you are referring. In the passage to which you object, I attacked the basic concept of postmodernism, which claims that the "modernist" project based on the belief in the possibility of human progress – dating back to the Enlightenment and lasting through much of the 20th century – ended in failure. Your response to this passage in my lecture can only signify that you identify with the positions that I am criticizing. However, you fail to state which defenders of the Enlightenment heritage of reason and confidence in the possibility of human progress you consider reactionary and which of its opponents you consider progressive. And, may I ask, in which of the writings of the great Marxists will one find either condemnation of Enlightenment thinkers or praise for their opponents?

In a manner that crudely suggests that the Reason of the Enlightenment thinkers merely provided rationalizations for class oppression, your passage conflates into one undifferentiated and ahistorical process the mighty theoretical struggles that laid the intellectual foundations for the great bourgeois revolutions of the 18th century and the socio-economic reality of the bourgeois-capitalistic societies that emerged eventually from those upheavals. However, whatever the historically-conditioned illusions of the Enlightenment thinkers – specifically, that the liberation of the "third estate" represented the liberation of all mankind – their theoretical work ultimately provided the intellectual and, one might add (though within certain limits), moral basis for the socialist assault on bourgeois society. The revolutionary thinkers of the 17th and 18th centuries forged the weapons that were ultimately to be used by the new socialist movement and emerging working class against bourgeois society in the 19th century. It was the betrayal of the ideals of reason by the bourgeoisie in the aftermath of the French Revolution that provided so much of the theoretical impulse for the critique of bourgeois society. Moreover, your claim that the Enlightenment philosophers provided "rationalizations of a new form of class oppression" is grotesquely one-sided and basically false. You simply ignore the implicitly communist theories advanced by Enlightenment thinkers, and seem to be unaware that the materialist philosophy of the Enlightenment, notwithstanding its limitations, tended in the direction of the repudiation of property and inequality. As Marx pointed out in his commentary on French 18th century materialism in *The Holy Family*:

> There is no need for any great penetration to see from the teaching of materialism on the original goodness and equal endowment of men, the omnipotence of experience, habit and education, and the influence of environment on man, the great significance of industry, the justification of enjoyment, etc., how necessarily materialism is connected with communism and socialism. [*Marx Engels Collected Works*, Volume 4 (New York, 1975), p. 130]

Your reference to the "reason" of bourgeois society – which you call upon Marxists to fight – is confused and misleading. In the course of the historical development of bourgeois society and the growth of class antagonisms, the bourgeoisie tended more and more to abandon "Reason" in favor of increasingly subjective and irrationalist philosophies. The decline of Hegel's stature in the aftermath of the failed 1848-49 Revolutions, and his replacement by Schopenhauer and later Nietzsche as the towering figures of philosophy, represented the bourgeois repudiation of Reason. Thus, the great Marxists have always claimed to represent the revolutionary heritage of the Reason of the Enlightenment, understanding by that term the capacity of man, acting on the basis of a scientific insight into the laws of nature and society, to put an end to exploitation, oppression and injustice. It is this heritage that Trotsky invoked at the conclusion of his great oration before the Commission of Inquiry, chaired by American philosopher John Dewey, into the Moscow Trial charges:

> Esteemed Commissioners! The experience of my life, in which there has been no lack of successes or failures, has not only not destroyed my faith in the clear, bright future of mankind, but, on the contrary, has given it an indestructible temper. This faith in reason, in truth, in human solidarity, which at the age of eighteen I took with me into the workers' quarters of the provincial Russian town of Nikolaiev – this faith I have preserved fully and completely. [*The Case of Leon Trotsky* (New York, 1969), pp. 584-85]

The tradition which you represent in your strictures against the Enlightenment traces its origins not to Marx, but to the demoralized petty-bourgeois theorists of the Frankfurt School – particularly, to the conceptions initially propounded by Max Horkheimer and Theodor Adorno in their *Dialectic of Enlightenment*. In this work, the Enlightenment of the 18th century is held accountable for the catastrophes of the 20th century. Human reason, science, technology and even social progress are listed as factors contributing to the triumph of fascism. The central arguments in *Dialectic of Enlightenment* were summed up in the lecture given last summer at Ann Arbor by Comrade Peter Schwarz. Your document makes no reference to his analysis. Throwing in terms like "dialectical negation" and "dialectical break" adds neither cogency nor profundity to your assault on the Enlightenment. Rather, it illustrates how you seek to exploit pseudo-Hegelian phraseology in the service of conceptions that are inimical to Marxism.

11. The origins of the campaign for "Utopia"

The purpose of your attempt to build a case against the International Committee is to show that our refusal to accept your pseudo-utopian enterprise as an essential component of the revolutionary program is the product "of the deadening effect of objectivism on the fight for socialist class consciousness." Not only that, my "strident condemnation of utopianism" demonstrates that "Marxism continues to be plagued by a spurious and reductive materialism that 'disdains the human factors' and denigrates the struggle for socialist class consciousness."

It is at this point necessary to retrace the path, extending back over nearly a decade, which led you to this damning indictment of the International Committee and of my own theoretical and political outlook.

The first serious indication that we were moving along different political trajectories emerged in 1998, when you, Comrade Brenner, submitted to the *World Socialist Web Site* a lengthy article on the subject of sexuality and gender identity that we chose not to publish. The article seemed to us to be based on highly speculative and dubious propositions that minimized, if not entirely denied, the significance of biology in sexual orientation. There was no indication that the article was informed by a serious study of evolutionary biology or anthropology. Comrade Dave Walsh, who had reviewed the article, brought some of his concerns to your attention. To this you sent a lengthy reply, dated June 28, 1998, which not only failed to assuage our objections to your article, but raised in our own mind concerns about your new programmatic agenda.

Your letter informed us that it was urgently necessary to develop "an alternative theory of gender," that "this would have a profound effect on any socialist project to restructure the family," that "the stakes for Marxists on this issue are considerable," and that "our position on this kind of question can help – or hinder – our effort to win support for making the revolution."

Until your letter had arrived, it had not occurred to any of us that there was any pressing need for a "socialist project to restructure the family," let alone a new conception of gender or "a Marxist theory of sexuality." Moreover, the style of Comrade Brenner's letter – written in a manner that seemed self-consciously and immaturely intent on shocking the reader – was distinctly deficient in literary aesthetics.[13] But worst of all,

---

13 A few characteristic passages: "Thus, if we contend that biology provides an impetus to genital sex, we must also be willing to admit that biology provides an impetus to oral sex – which is of course a type of sex that can be gratified by either gender. And, for that matter, in shifting libido to the penis, biology doesn't at the same time compel the penis to seek gratification only in the vagina: on the contrary, the mouth and anus --- again, of either gender, will do as well, to say nothing of masturbation." And: "Surely, there is nothing mature or fully developed about a genital

the letter did not offer a single citation from a scientific text to bolster its own extravagant and lurid arguments.

Although we heard informally that you were dissatisfied with our refusal to publish your article on gender, it was not until 2002 that new differences emerged. On May 30, 2002, the *World Socialist Web Site* posted a letter that Comrade Nick Beams, the national secretary of the Socialist Equality Party in Australia and member of the International Editorial Board of the *WSWS*, had written in response to questions raised by a reader about the nature of life under socialism. The questions touched on a range of issues, including the relationship between economic efficiency and full employment, the problem of individual motivation and initiative, the future of small business, the forms of governmental decision-making, the precise location of a future world capital, the moral basis of socialist society, and the impact of socialism on the family, human rights and the ecology. The questions were typical of those which arise in political discussions with people who are just being introduced to socialism. While such questions certainly deserve a serious reply, Marxists also understand that it is important to explain, in the interests of theoretical and political clarification, that socialism does not consist of a series of prescriptions laid down in advance. It is not that we decline, under all circumstances, to speculate about the future under socialism. But, as historical materialists, we understand the limits of such speculation, which must, at any rate, base itself on a profound analysis of the real contradictions of the capitalist mode of production and the social relations to which it gives rise. Moreover, a socialist society is one whose

---

sexuality in which the sexual act consists solely of a man mounting a woman and thrusting his penis into her vagina until ejaculation; on the contrary, this kind of behavior is clearly a mark of extreme repression, of the constriction of sexuality to a mechanical, inhuman coldness."

fundamental features will emerge as an expression of the self-emancipation of the working class, rather than in accordance with a schema worked out by leaders in advance.

Beams argued along these lines when asked to draw a picture of the future socialist society. [See http://www.wsws.org/articles/2002/may2002/corr-m30.shtml] "The development of a socialist society," he wrote, "will not take place according to a series of prescriptions and rules laid down by an individual, a political party or a government authority. Rather, it will develop on the basis of the activity of the members of society, who for the first time in history will consciously regulate their own social organization as part of their daily lives, free from the domination and prescriptions of either the free market or a bureaucratic authority standing over them." Nick also stressed that the material precondition for a society that strives to realize genuine human emancipation "is the development of the social productivity of labor to such a point that the vast bulk of humanity does not have to spend the greater portion of the day merely trying to obtain the resources to maintain itself. The great contribution of capitalism to the advance of human civilization is that, through its continuous development of the productive forces and the productivity of labor, it has created the necessary material foundations for such genuine human emancipation." Beams then briefly outlined how, on the basis of these material foundations, a socialist society might tackle some of the economic and social questions raised in the correspondent's letter. But in relation to the issue of morality, Beams noted that "Marxism has always rejected the attempt to impose some moral dogma, pointing out that, inasmuch as society has always been divided into classes, morality is a class issue. Moral values either justify the interests of the ruling stratum or represent the interests of the oppressed classes. When class society is abolished, a new morality will develop." This response was not, obviously, intended as the final word on the subject of Marxism and morality. It was, however, adequate and correct in the context of a brief letter written in response to a reader's questions. Similarly, on the issue of the family, a subject of vast complexity, Nick confined himself to stating, correctly, that "socialist society will have no prescriptions. However, people will have the material means to freely enter into those relationships that they find meaningful."

Comrade Brenner, you then wrote a letter dated July 24, 2002 registering your strong disagreement with the manner in which Beams had replied to the reader's questions. "From Beams's reply," you wrote, "it is impossible to get a sense of where Utopia is in the outlook of contemporary Marxism." The short answer to this question – though it is not one that you wanted to hear – is that Utopia is precisely where it is supposed to be in a serious revolutionary program that bases itself on an analysis of the socio-economic foundations of capitalism and the laws of historical development: *that is, it is not part of a Marxist program*. We shall amplify on this point somewhat later; but first we must return to your letter. Protesting that Beams failed to properly answer the reader, you declared: "All his [the reader's] questions are in essence one question: What would socialists do if they ran society? Surely a movement that calls for a revolution has to have a convincing answer to that question, and that means policies on a wide gamut of social issues and a clear vision of the kind of society this revolutionary program is meant to bring about. Otherwise there is something unserious about the call for revolution."

The suggestion that the Fourth International and its sections lack a program, that we are missing policies "on a wide gamut of social issues," and that our movement calls for revolution without having any clear sense of what kind of society we propose as an alternative to capitalism, is totally unfounded. There is no party whose record of programmatic statements

is as comprehensive as that of the International Committee
of the Fourth International.[14] When you accused the ICFI of
lacking a program, what you really meant is that the Marxist

---

14 A comprehensive collection of documents in which the programmatic record of the Fourth International and its sections was presented
(dating back to 1938) would run into dozens of volumes. For the sake of
brevity, I will cite only one example of our programmatic position, which
is taken from the report I delivered in June 1995 proposing the transformation of the Workers League into the Socialist Equality Party:

> The aim of our party should be stated clearly in its name and in
> a manner that the workers can both understand and identify with.
> I propose at this time that we initiate preparations for the transfor-
> mation of the Workers League into the Socialist Equality Party.
> Briefly, in presenting this party to the working class, we must ex-
> plain that its goal is the establishment of a workers' government:
> and by that we mean a government for the workers, of the workers
> and by the workers. Such a government will utilize the political
> power it intends to gain through democratic means, if possible,
> to reorganize economic life in the interests of the working class,
> to overcome and replace the socially-destructive market forces of
> capitalism with democratic social planning, to undertake a radical
> reorganization of production to meet the urgent social needs of the
> working people, to effect a radical and socially-just redistribution
> of wealth in favor of the working population, and thereby lay the
> basis for socialism.
> We will stress that these aims of the Socialist Equality Party are
> realizable only in alliance with, and as an integral part of, a con-
> sciously internationalist movement of the working class. There
> cannot be social equality and social justice for the American
> worker as long as multinational and transnational corporations op-
> press and exploit his class brothers and sisters in other countries.
> Moreover, there exists no viable national strategy upon which the
> class struggle can be based. The working class must consistently
> and systematically counterpose its international strategy to the in-
> ternational strategy of the transnational corporations. There can be
> no compromise on this essential question, which is the cutting edge
> of the socialist program.

conception of program and its relationship to the struggle for working class power contradicts your own. You believe, as we shall see, that the revolutionary movement should issue "socialist" encyclicals on subjects and issues that fall well outside the boundaries of a political program, such as the appropriate form of the post-revolutionary family and the nature of sexuality under communism. Comrade Brenner, you are not particularly interested in the formulation of demands whose content is rooted in the objective contradictions of bourgeois society and which express the political and socio-economic interests of the working class in its struggle against capitalist

---

In striving to politically organize the working class, the Socialist Equality Party must respond to the pressing needs of the masses that arise out of existing social conditions. At a time when international capital is engaged in an unrelenting offensive against the working class, the social demands which address the basic needs of the working class assume a revolutionary character. After all, the old organizations would not have abandoned reformist demands if it were possible to achieve them through reformist measures. Every demand of the working class, on the most basic questions, poses a direct confrontation between the working class and the capitalist state.

We must outline, in detail, the demands which we will incorporate into our program. It is not necessary, however, to write a program as if it were a blueprint for the socialist utopia of the future. Rather, it must provide the working class with a unifying aim that corresponds to its objective interests. Moreover, it must strike a chord in the consciousness of the masses. The demand for social equality not only sums up the basic aim of the socialist movement; it also evokes the egalitarian traditions that are so deeply rooted in the genuinely democratic and revolutionary traditions of the American workers. All the great social struggles of American history have inscribed on their banners the demand for social equality. It is no accident that today, in the prevailing environment of political reaction, this ideal is under relentless attack. [For the entire report, see http://www.wsws.org/sections/category/icfi/wlsep.shtml]

oppression, exploitation and inequality. Rather, you conceive of program as, to quote your letter, "a socialist dream, in which socialism and a happy life become associated in the minds of millions of people." This constitutes the essential foundation of your call for a revival of Utopianism.

When Beams replied to Brenner's complaint on August 29, 2002, he focused on one critical issue: "The point I was making and to which you so strenuously object, is that socialist society is not one which is run by socialists. Rather, it is a form of society in which the working class, the overwhelming majority of the population, for the first time in history takes economic and political power in its hands. There is one very important conception here: The emancipation of labor is not to be worked out in a series of prescriptions handed down from some authority but must be worked out by the masses themselves."

In response to this letter from Nick Beams, you produced your manifesto on Utopia. The purpose of this document, you (Comrade Brenner) informed us, was two-fold: first, to correct "seriously misguided" conceptions about the relationship between Marxism and utopianism; and, second, to examine "the tension between science and utopianism that turned the latter into a virtual taboo" within the Marxist movement. Having warned us that a "definitive account of all these matters would require a book-length discussion," you limited your treatment of these issues to a mere 27,393 words. This, you assured us, was "sufficient to make the case that a renewed attention to utopianism is vital to a rebirth of socialist culture within the working class."

12. Marx, Engels and utopianism

As we have already noted, you claim that Beams' "seriously misguided" views on utopianism are "indicative of prevailing (and longstanding) opinion within the Marxist movement…"

Beams' errors, moreover, arise from "the tension between science and utopianism that turned the latter into a virtual taboo." You state that Beams is the latest in a long line of revisionists, dating back to the Second International in the late 19th century, who have falsely claimed that Marx and Engels were hostile to utopianism in order to advance their own anti-revolutionary reformist agendas. Citing an extract from *The Civil War in France* (which Marx wrote in 1871 in defense of the Paris Commune), you assert:

> The relationship between utopianism and Marxism as it is presented in this passage is markedly different from the way that relationship is usually presented by Marxists. By the latter I mean essentially the view that once Marxism had made socialism into a science, utopianism became irrelevant. The primary text on which this view is based is Engels' *Socialism: Utopian and Scientific*, and there is no question that there, as elsewhere, both he and Marx subjected utopian socialism to a profound critique that was crucial to the whole project of a scientific socialism. But that critique didn't render utopianism irrelevant, any more than the advent of Marxism rendered Hegel's philosophy or Smith and Ricardo's political economy irrelevant.

Your introduction of the word "irrelevant" is a terminological sleight of hand. The issue is not whether the ideas of the great utopian socialists are "irrelevant." Nick Beams did not make such a statement. "Irrelevant" is not a word that students of intellectual history apply to works of great thinkers of the past. Every new generation of thinkers stands on the foundations laid down by those who preceded them. A deep understanding of Marxism requires the *critical* assimilation of the entire antecedent history of socialist thought, from Plato to the utopians of the late 18th and early 19th century. However, an appreciation of the contribution of past thinkers does not mean that their theories can be utilized, in their historically given form, in contemporary conditions.

Marx and Engels acknowledged on numerous occasions the immense intellectual debt that modern *scientific* socialism owed to the great utopians Saint-Simon, Fourier and Owen. They also explained at great length the historically-conditioned character and limitations of their predecessors' contributions. As Engels wrote, the utopians "were utopians because they could be nothing else at a time when capitalist production was as yet so little developed. They necessarily had to construct the elements of a new society out of their own heads, because within the old society the elements of the new were not as yet generally apparent; for the basic plan of the new evidence they could only appeal to reason, just because as yet they could not appeal to contemporary history." [*Marx-Engels Collected Works*, Volume 25 (New York: 1987), p. 253]

Your claim that the views of Marx and Engels on the subject of utopianism have been misrepresented by subsequent generations – that is, that their supposed hostility to utopianism has been exaggerated – is without foundation. Anyone who has access to their *Collected Works* can easily locate innumerable citations in which their critical attitude toward utopianism is precisely formulated. Paying necessary respect to its contribution to the development of socialism, they insisted that utopianism belonged to the past, not the present or the future, of the revolutionary socialist movement. This is the very point that is made in the passage from *The Civil War in France* that you quote. How you, Comrade Brenner, can claim that this passage supports your potted interpretation of Marxism is beyond me. It explains that the epoch of utopianism ended precisely at the point when the maturation of capitalism brought the working class into existence as a revolutionary force. The position is made even more explicit when one includes the four sentences that precede the extract that you cite:

> All the Socialist founders of Sects belong to a period in which the working class were neither sufficiently trained and organized by the march of capitalist society itself to enter as historical actors upon the world's stage, nor were the material conditions of their emancipation sufficiently matured in the old world itself. Their misery existed, but the conditions of their own movement did not yet exist. The utopian founders of sects, while in their criticism of present society clearly describing the goal of the social movement, the supersession of the wages system with all its economic conditions of class rule, found neither in society itself the material conditions of its transformation nor in the working class the organized power and the conscience of the movement. They tried to compensate for the historical conditions of the movement by fantastic pictures and plans of a new society in whose propaganda they saw the true means of salvation. [*Marx-Engels Collected Works*, Volume 22 (New York, 1986), p. 499]

It is at this point that you pick up the citation:

> From the moment the workingmen class movement became real, the fantastic utopias evanesced, not because the working class had given up the end aimed at by these Utopists, but because they had found the real means to realize them, but in their place came a real insight into the historic conditions of the movement and a more and more gathering force of the military organization of the working class. But the last two ends of the movement proclaimed by the Utopians are the

last ends proclaimed by the Paris Revolution and by
the International. Only the means are different and the
real conditions of the movement are no longer clouded
in utopian fables. [Ibid. pp. 499-500]

To all those who can understand what they read, it is per-
fectly clear that Marx is arguing that utopianism belongs to
an earlier stage in the development of socialism, one that has
been overtaken and superseded by the development of capitalism and the emergence of a mass working class.

For Marx, the Paris Commune represented the supreme
historical substantiation of the struggle he had waged over
nearly 30 years, in opposition to myriad forms of utopianism,
to place socialist theory on a scientific basis. The theoretical
work of Marx and Engels between 1843 and 1847 – whose
greatest achievement was the critique of Hegelian idealism
and, on this basis, the elaboration of the materialist conception of history – laid down the philosophical and political
foundations of the modern socialist movement. This period
of intense intellectual labor culminated in the writing of *The
Communist Manifesto*. During the next 20 years, Marx devoted his energies almost entirely to the scientific substantiation
of the revolutionary perspective that it advanced. This substantiation consisted principally of 1) the successful utilization of the materialist conception of history as an instrument
of political analysis (making possible the demystification and
rational comprehension of political developments, such as
the notorious coup d'etat that established the dictatorship of
Louis Bonaparte); and 2) the discovery of the economic laws
governing the motion of capitalist society, culminating in the
publication of the first volume of *Capital* in 1867.[15]

---

15 The most splendid narration of the origins of Marxism is to be
found in Engels' *Socialism: Utopian and Scientific*. I will resist the tempta-

tion to reproduce the text in its entirety, and cite only the most relevant passage:

> Hegel had freed history from metaphysics – he had made it dialectic; but his conception of history was essentially idealistic. But now idealism was driven from its last refuge, the philosophy of history; now a materialistic treatment of history was propounded, and a method found of explaining man's 'knowing' by his 'being,' instead of, as heretofore, his 'being' by his 'knowing.'
>
> From that time forward Socialism was no longer an accidental discovery of this or that ingenious brain, but the necessary outcome of the struggle between two historically developed classes – the proletariat and the bourgeoisie. Its task was no longer to manufacture a system of society as perfect as possible, but to examine the historico-economic succession of events from which these classes and their antagonism had of necessity sprung, and to discover in the economic conditions thus created the means of ending the conflict. But the Socialism of earlier days was as incompatible with this materialistic conception as the conception of Nature of the French materialists was with dialectics and natural science. The Socialism of earlier days certainly criticized the existing capitalistic mode of production and its consequences. But it could not explain them, and, therefore, could not get the mastery of them. It could only simply reject them as bad. The more strongly this earlier Socialism denounced the exploitation of the working-class, inevitable under Capitalism, the less able was it clearly to show in what this exploitation consisted and how it arose. But for this it was necessary -- (1) to present the capitalistic method of production in its historical connection and its inevitableness during a particular historical period, and therefore, also, to present its inevitable downfall; and (2) to lay bare its essential character, which was still a secret. This was done by the discovery of *surplus-value*. It was shown that the appropriation of unpaid labor is the basis of the capitalist mode of production and of the exploitation of the worker that occurs under it; and even if the capitalist buys the labor-power of his laborer at its full value as a commodity on the market, he yet extracts more value from it than he paid for; and that in the ultimate analysis this surplus-value forms those sums of value from which are heaped

During the early years of the German Social Democratic Party, Marx and Engels were brutally critical of any tendency that expressed a retreat from these theoretical conquests. In the climate of political reaction that followed the suppression of the Commune and the consolidation of Bismarck's German empire, they had to contend repeatedly with political-ideological currents that sought to revive antiquated doctrines that Marx and Engels had refuted decades earlier. On October 19, 1877, Marx penned an angry complaint to his friend Friedrich Adolph Sorge, who was living in Hoboken, New Jersey.

> In Germany a corrupt spirit is asserting itself in our party, not so much among the masses as among the leaders (upperclass and "workers"). The compromise with the Lassalleans has led to further compromise with other waverers; in Berlin (via *Most*) with Dühring and his "admirers," not to mention a whole swarm of immature undergraduates and over-wise graduates who want to give socialism a "higher idealistic" orientation, i.e., substitute for the materialist basis (which calls for serious, objective study if one is to operate thereon) a modern mythology with its goddesses of Justice, Liberty, Equality and Fraternité. Dr. Höchberg[16], the

---

up the constantly increasing masses of capital in the hands of the possessing classes. The genesis of capitalist production and the production of capital were both explained.

These two great discoveries, the materialistic conception of history and the revelation of the secret of capitalistic production through surplus-value, we owe to Marx. With these discoveries Socialism became a science. The next thing was to work out all its details and relations. [*Marx-Engels Collected Works*, Volume 24, (London, 1989), p. 305]

16 Karl Höchberg (1853-1885) was a wealthy supporter of the socialist movement.

gentlemen who edits the *Zukunft* [Future], is a representative of this tendency and has "bought his way" into the party − no doubt with the "noblest" of intentions, but I don't give a fig for "intentions." Seldom has anything more pitiful than his program for the *Zukunft* been ushered into the world with more "modest pretensions."

The workers themselves, when like Mr. Most and Co. they give up working and become *literati by profession*, invariably wreak "theoretical" havoc and are always ready to consort with addle-heads of the supposedly "learned" caste. In particular, what we had been at such pains to eject from the German workers' heads decades ago, thereby ensuring their theoretical (and hence also practical) ascendancy over the French and English, − namely *Utopian* socialism, the play of the imagination on the future structure of society, − is once again rampant and in a far more ineffectual form, not only as compared with the great French and English Utopians, but with − Weitling.[17] It stands to reason that Utopianism which bore within itself the seeds of critical and materialist socialism, *before* the advent of the latter, can now, *post festum*, only seem silly, stale and thoroughly reactionary. [*Marx-Engels Collected Works*, Volume 45 (Moscow, 1991), pp. 283-84.]

This passage is a concise summation of Marx's estimate of efforts to reintroduce utopianism into the socialist movement. Yes, it is true that Beams' disavowal of utopianism represents,

---

17 Wilhelm Weitling (1808-1871) was one of the earliest leaders of the young workers' movement in Germany in the late 1830s and 1840s. He promoted a form of utopian communism that Engels described as "sentimental Love-mongering."

as you, Comrade Brenner, state, "prevailing (and longstanding) opinion within the Marxist movement." But if this "opinion" is "misguided," your differences are, first and foremost, with Marx and Engels rather than with Nick Beams.

13. The idealist method of utopianism

Ideas develop in accordance with a certain historically-determined logic. As a product of their time, the conceptions of the great *progressive* utopians of the late 18th and early 19th centuries were grounded in the materialist philosophy of that epoch. But that materialism was of a primarily mechanical, static and ahistorical character, and therefore could not account adequately for the development of social consciousness. The limitation of this form of materialism found its most significant expression in the utopians' conception of the relationship between consciousness and the realization of the social ideals that they advocated. The French materialists of the late 18th century insisted that man is a product of his social environment. Both his virtues and vices arose from this objective source; and, therefore, it was only through changes in his social environment that man's virtues could be multiplied and his vices eliminated. Thus, alterations in consciousness required the alteration of the social environment within which man's consciousness developed. But this raised a further question: how was this social environment to be changed? It was here that the French materialists found themselves trapped within a conundrum from which their philosophy offered no escape. Man is a product of his environment. But the social environment, they argued, is a product of ... public opinion! Where did this conclusion leave the materialists of the 18th century? If man is a product of his social environment, it would seem to follow that public opinion itself is a product of that environment. Yet, the materialists turned the argument around and made the social environment a product of public opinion! And so, notwithstanding the essentially materialist foundations of their epistemology, the French *philosophes* arrived at the idealist conclusion that changes in the social environment depended principally upon changes in thought, or, as the French materialists often posed the issue, in "human nature."

Within the framework of French materialism, no solution could be found to the Social Environment – Public Opinion conundrum. Rather, a solution depended upon the discovery of objective forces, not dependent upon "public opinion," that both determined the social environment and shaped the form and direction of social consciousness. The discovery of such objective forces was the singular achievement of the materialist conception of history elaborated by Marx and Engels.

What has all this to do with your document, Comrade Brenner? In pleading for the revival of utopianism, you more or less reproduce the theoretical conundrum that bedeviled the materialists of the 18th century. But while their errors had the charm of originality and genius, yours, 250 years later, appear merely foolish. "The central point I am making," you write, "is that it is just because the proletariat is the only conceivable revolutionary subject of history that utopia is important: *class consciousness will never be revived until socialism becomes once again a great social ideal*, the focal point for the aspirations and dreams of the broad mass of workers, young people and intellectuals." [Emphasis added]

Let us examine this argument with the attention it deserves: "Class consciousness will never be revived until socialism becomes once again a great social ideal." But the emergence of socialism as "the focal point for the aspirations and dreams of the broad mass of workers, young people and intellectuals" could only mean that a colossal development of class consciousness had already occurred. Stripped down to its naked

essentials, your formula makes the revival of class consciousness dependent upon the revival of ideals, that is, upon one of
the aspects or components of class consciousness. You might
just as well have written that "Socialism (as an especially advanced expression of class consciousness) will never be revived
until socialism becomes once again a great social ideal." We are
left with a tautology. You fail to answer the obvious question:
how will socialism become a "great social ideal"? Do there exist
objective conditions independent of consciousness that will
provide a real socio-economic impulse for that development?
For all your invective against mechanical materialism, you reproduce the fundamental flaws of that mode of thought.

The mechanical character of 18th century materialism, which
made a relapse into an idealist conception of the development of
social consciousness unavoidable, was historically conditioned
by the existing level of socio-economic and scientific-technolog-
ical development. Neither industrial capitalism nor the working class had matured to the point required for the discovery
that the development of the productive forces and the social
relations to which they give rise comprise the real and objective
foundation of social consciousness. Socialist thought assumed
a utopian character precisely because historical conditions did
not yet exist for establishing the link between social consciousness and the objective development of socio-economic forces.
Moreover, precisely because the utopians were unable to identify the objective source of changes in consciousness, the process
of changing consciousness could only be conceived of in terms
of education carried out by enlightened individuals.

By the 1840s there had been a considerable development of
both capitalism and the working class in Britain, France and
Germany. It became possible to identify the objective forces,
operating in relative independence of peoples' thinking, which
underlay dramatic changes in social consciousness and generated immense eruptions of open class conflict. In the face

of these developments, conceptions which made fundamental shifts in social consciousness dependent upon the pedagogical efforts of advanced and isolated thinkers assumed an ever-more apparent reactionary character. In Germany, such conceptions were associated with a tendency known as the critical critics, whose principal representative was Bruno Bauer. Analyzing this tendency, Plekhanov wrote:

> "Opinion governs the world" – thus declared the writers of the French Enlightenment. Thus also spoke, as we see, the Bauer brothers when they revolted against Hegelian idealism. But if opinion governs the world, then the prime movers of history are now those men whose thought criticizes the old and creates the new opinions. The Bauer brothers did in fact think so. The essence of the historical process reduced itself, in their view, to the refashioning by the "critical spirit" of the existing store of opinions, and of the forms of life in society conditioned by that store...
>
> Once having imagined himself to be the main architect, the Demiurge of history, the "critically thinking" man thereby separates off himself and those like him into a special, higher variety of the human race. This higher variety is contrasted to the *mass*, foreign to critical thought, and capable only of playing the part of clay in the creative hands of "critically thinking" personalities. [*The Development of the Monist View of History* (Moscow, 1974), pp. 118-19]

14. Socialists and the masses

Proceeding on the basis of similar idealist conceptions, you, Comrade Brenner, arrive at a conception of the relationship between socialists and the masses that resembles to a remark-able degree the position of the "critical critics" as summarized above by Plekhanov.

"According to Beams," you write, "it will not be socialists but the masses who will run socialist society, and so there is no need for socialist policies – which he refers to disparagingly as 'prescriptions' – on issues like the family, work, the environment, etc., let alone a coherent vision of what socialist society will be like. There is a basic truth here – that the working class must emancipate itself – which is fundamental to the socialist project. But never before has this been interpreted to mean that socialists don't need to have a program."

Once again, you resort to a polemical sleight of hand: Beams' statement that a socialist society is not one "run" by socialists and that it is the task of the working class, in the process of its self-emancipation, to work out the new forms of society, with-out "prescriptions" laid down in advance, is misrepresented as a repudiation of program.

You insist that "there is no contradiction between the masses emancipating themselves and socialists running so-ciety." Are the masses to assume that this is the case because you, Commissar Brenner, say so? Either the self-emancipa-tion of the working class means that it is the masses who must create and work out the forms of their own liberation or it does not. This is not merely an issue of abstract theo-retical interest. The question has merely to be posed: Would a revolutionary socialist government, in the aftermath of the conquest of political power, be subject to the democratic con-trol of the working class? Would the working out of policies proceed on the basis of diktats issued by the ruling socialists or through the open struggle among diverse social tenden-cies, whose right to fight for their viewpoints and policies would be among the most precious and zealously defended of democratic rights?

One has only to read your description of the state of affairs in the aftermath of the revolution to imagine your reply to these questions:

> Some workers will actively oppose the revolution: to imagine them running anything in a socialist society is perverse. Others will be politically neutral: to foist responsibilities on them right away for a revolution they have barely begun to understand will probably do little more than antagonize them; their political consciousness (and more broadly, their general cultural level) will have to be patiently nurtured. So for a considerable period of time the running of socialist society will be in the hands, not of the amorphous "masses," but of class conscious workers – in other words, that section of the class (necessarily a large portion of it and hopefully a majority) whose political consciousness has been shaped by the revolutionary socialist movement. This, it needs to be emphasized, is what is meant by "socialists running society" – not a small clique of party bureaucrats but a broad section of workers imbued with socialist consciousness.

One doesn't know whether to laugh or to cry as one reads your vision of the situation with which a socialist government will be confronted. Though you hold out the hope that a majority of the working class (though clearly not the majority of the population as a whole) will support the revolution, there seems to be no question in your mind that the socialists will be spending at least as much time suppressing people as they will emancipating them. Moreover, if all those sections of the working class from whom you anticipate opposition or indifference are to be excluded from "running anything," the continued functioning of a substantial portion of the economic, technological and social infrastructure of an advanced society will be, to put it mildly, problematic. There are limits to what can be decided on the basis of purely political considerations. In the aftermath of winning power, a socialist workers' government will require the interested cooperation of large numbers of people who, whatever their political convictions, will continue to play critical roles in the infrastructure of society. Socialists, even if they were so inclined, could not simply order these people about. They will have to be not only listened to, but also treated with the respect that their experience and expertise merits.

Fixated as you are on conjuring up prescriptions for the socialist society of the future, it does not seem that you have given too much thought to the problems of the transition from capitalism to socialism. By its very nature, socialism is inconceivable without mass participation in the making of decisions on all issues affecting the lives of the people, that is, without a vast expansion in democracy. As Engels put the matter so well, in his May 1895 Introduction to a new edition of Karl Marx's *The Class Struggle in France* (completed just three months before his own death): "The time of surprise attacks, of revolutions carried through by small conscious minorities at the head of masses lacking consciousness is past. Where it is a question of a complete transformation of the social organization, the masses themselves must also be in on it, must have already grasped what is at stake, what they are fighting for, body and soul. The history of the last fifty years has taught us that." [*Marx-Engels Collected Works*, Volume 27, (Moscow 1990), p. 520]

In others words, the revolution cannot be made *for* the workers. It must be made *by* the workers who understand what they are fighting for. The conception that the working class is capable of fighting for, and winning, political power can appear reasonable only to those who believe that masses of workers will be drawn to the perspective of socialism out of the experiences of their own lives. But you, Comrade Brenner, do not believe this. All that you see in the masses is a spectacle of appalling backwardness. You write: "If by the sheer act of participating in a revolution the undifferentiated masses can, as it were, leap out of their skins and transcend a lifetime of oppression and backwardness to the point of being able to carry out the mammoth task of socialist construction *on their own*, i.e., without any guidance or 'prescriptions' from socialists, then one has to wonder why they would need these same socialists to lead them in making a revolution in the first place. One has to wonder, in short, why they would need a *change* in consciousness at all."

Backward the workers come into the revolution. Backward they leave it. Only through the Herculean efforts of Frank Brenner can something be salvaged from this general mess and the masses led, despite themselves, to the new utopia.

15. Consciousness and socialism

Fortunately, the real historical process proceeds quite differently. The change in social consciousness that necessarily precedes the outbreak of revolution as well as its subsequent evolution in the course of great struggles is rooted in and is the expression of socio-economic processes that develop independently of individual consciousness. Moreover, the immense "leaps" in consciousness characteristic of a period of revolutionary struggle represent the long-postponed (and therefore explosive) realignment of social thought with external social reality.[18] The experience of mass struggles changes people and

---

18 This process was explained by Trotsky as follows: "The swift changes in mass views and moods in an epoch of revolution thus derive,

their consciousness. Or as Marx and Engels put it when reply-
ing to the Brenners of the 1840s:

> Both for the production on a mass scale of this com-
> munist consciousness and for the success of the cause it-
> self, the alteration of men on a mass scale is necessary, an
> alteration which can only take place in a practical move-
> ment, a *revolution*; the revolution is necessary, therefore,
> not only because the *ruling* class cannot be overthrown
> in any other way, but also because the class *overthrowing*
> it can only in a revolution succeed in ridding itself of the
> muck of ages and become fitted to found society anew.
> [*Marx-Engels Collected Works*, Volume 5 (New York,
> 1976), pp. 52-53, emphasis in the original]

This justly celebrated passage appears in *The German
Ideology*, written jointly by Marx and Engels in 1845. This
work represented the first elaboration of the materialist conception of history, which explained man's social consciousness
on the basis of his social being, rather than man's being on the
basis of his consciousness. The forms of man's thinking, they
discovered, develop on an objective, material basis. "It is not
consciousness that determines life, but life that determines
consciousness." [ibid. p. 37] Their new conception of history
and the development of consciousness "relies on expounding
the real process of production – starting from the material
production of life itself – and comprehending the form of in-

---

not from the flexibility and mobility of man's mind, but just the opposite, from its deep conservativism. The chronic lag of ideas and relations
behind new objective conditions, right up to the moment when the latter
crash over people in the form of a catastrophe, is what creates in a period
of revolution that leaping movement of ideas and passions which seems
to the police mind a mere result of the activities of 'demagogues.'" [*The
History of the Russian Revolution* (London, 1977), p. 18]

tercourse connected with and created by this mode of production, i.e., civil society in its various stages, as the basis of all history…" [ibid. p. 53]

The conception of social revolution as an objective product of real socio-economic contradictions in the emerging capitalist system dealt a death-blow to all idealist interpretations of history. Moreover, the development of the working class itself as a revolutionary force within society, the "gravedigger" of capitalism, was an objective process. Its world-historical role was determined, in the most fundamental sense, not by its consciousness, but rather by its unique position in the capitalist mode of production. Answering what was to prove to be the most enduring objections to the conception of the proletariat as a revolutionary force – that the working class lacked revolutionary consciousness, that it did not want revolution, etc. – Marx and Engels replied in *The Holy Family*:

> It is not a question of what this or that proletarian, or even the whole proletariat, at the moment *regards* as its aim. It is a question of what the proletariat is, and what, in accordance with this being, it will historically be compelled to do. Its aim and historical action is visibly and irrevocably foreshadowed in its own life situation as well as in the whole organization of bourgeois society today. [*Marx-Engels Collected Works*, Volume 4 (New York, 1975), p. 37, emphasis in the original]

All Marxist discussion on the role of consciousness – a topic which, we should point out, in case you, Comrade Brenner, have not noticed, has been of considerable interest to the Trotskyist movement – must proceed from a correct understanding of its relationship to material processes of socio-economic development. Plans for the building of a revolutionary party and the development of socialist consciousness would come to nothing if there did not exist objective conditions permitting the realization of these goals. The elaboration of the materialist conception of history marked a gigantic advance in man's comprehension of his own social practice and consciousness. As Engels explained, "the final causes of all social changes and political revolutions are to be sought, not in men's brains, not in man's better insight into eternal truth and justice, but in changes in the modes of production and exchange. They are to be sought, not in the *philosophy*, but in the *economics* of each particular epoch." [*Marx-Engels Collected Works*, Volume 24 (London, 1989), p. 306] Even the emergence of a general "feeling" within broad sections of society that "things must change" is a reflection in social consciousness of the archaic character of the prevailing political and economic system.[19]

---

19 As Engels further writes in *Socialism: Utopian and Scientific*:

The growing perception that existing social institutions are unreasonable and unjust, that reason has become unreason, and right wrong, is only proof that in the modes of production and exchange changes have silently taken place, with which the old social order, adapted to earlier economic conditions, is no longer in keeping. From this it also follows that the means of getting rid of the incongruities that have been brought to light, must also be present, in a more or less developed condition, within the changed modes of production themselves. These means are not to be invented by deduction from fundamental principles, but are to be discovered in the stubborn facts of the existing system of production. ...

...The new productive forces have already outgrown the capitalistic mode of using them. And this conflict between productive forces and modes of production is not a conflict engendered in the mind of man, like that between original sin and divine justice. It exists, in fact, objectively outside us, independently of the will and actions even of the men that have brought it on. Modern Socialism is nothing but the reflex, in thought, of this conflict in fact; its ideal reflection in the minds, first, of the class directly suffering under it, the working class. [ibid. pp. 306-07]

The recognition that the emergence of the socialist movement has an objective foundation does not diminish the importance of the struggle to develop socialist consciousness. Indeed, the clarification of the objective basis of socialism is itself a critical component of the theoretical education of the working class. But the correct formulation of the socialist movement's pedagogical tasks is possible only within the framework of an understanding that the contradictions of capitalism provide the principal and decisive impulse for the development of revolutionary consciousness.

The problem of socialist consciousness presents itself in one manner to those who recognize the latter as the ideal reflection of a real socio-economic process, and in quite another manner to those for whom no such objective and necessary relationship exists between the economic foundations of capitalist society and the formation of social thought. For the Marxists, the fight for socialist consciousness does not consist of convincing the broad mass of workers to conduct a struggle against capitalism. Rather, proceeding from a recognition of the inevitability of such struggles, arising out of the objectively exploitative process of surplus-value extraction, intensified by the deepening economic and social crisis of the capitalist system, the Marxist movement strives to develop, within the advanced sections of the working class, a scientific understanding of history as a law-governed process, a knowledge of the capitalist mode of production and the social relations to which it gives rise, and an insight into the real nature of the present crisis and its world-historical implications. It is a matter of transforming an unconscious historical process into a conscious political movement, of anticipating and preparing for the consequences of the intensification of the world capitalist crisis, of laying bare the logic of events, and formulating, strategically and tactically, the appropriate political response.

But for those who see no basis for socialism in the objective conditions created by capitalism itself, who have been demoralized by the experience of defeats and setbacks, and who neither understand the nature of the capitalist crisis nor perceive the revolutionary potential of the working class, the problem of transforming consciousness is posed in essentially ideal and even psychological terms. Insofar as there does not exist a real basis for socialist consciousness, the possibility for its development must be sought elsewhere. That is precisely why you, Comrades Brenner and Steiner, believe that "utopia is crucial to a revival of socialist culture."

16. Brenner on the family and backwardness

For you, Comrade Brenner, the principal source of the virtually insuperable obstacles to the building of a socialist movement is to be found in the traumatized state of the human psyche. The blame for this, you believe, lies with the impact of the family upon consciousness. Therefore, before any real progress can be made toward the development of socialist consciousness, a program to deal with this institution will have to be worked out and made the focus of party work. "One shouldn't have to argue over whether socialists need a policy on the family," you exclaim. "Since we are fighting to create a world where people can live fully human lives for the first time in history, it is obvious that this goal is inconceivable without an overhaul of the institution responsible for the socialization – i.e., humanization – of children, and where in class society the earliest and often the deepest wounds are inflicted on the human personality." The family represents "sexual oppression and backwardness." Beams' failure to address this supreme problem, you assert, "is simply incredible." While you assure us that "it isn't the business of socialists to dictate to people how to live their personal lives," you are nothing less than aghast that Beams "completely ignores the measures that need to be taken" to overcome the obstacles created by the family to the development of consciousness. Socialists, you insist, "should have a great many things to say about the family – from programmatic demands to fight backwardness and sexual oppression to educational material about the goal of a collective family and the nature of personal life under socialism."

Beams' failure to commit the revolutionary movement to the advocacy of an alternative to the existing nuclear family represents a form of "socialist 'laissez-faire.'" Rejecting Beams' statement that the future family "will develop on the basis of the constantly evolving forms of economic and social organization which will arise in socialist society," you reply: "The whole point of socialism, however, is that for the first time in history human beings will *consciously direct* those changes, including in the family."

The panacea that you offer is the "collective family," which will "make it possible for both children and parents to break out of what Wilhelm Reich once called 'family-itis,' that stifling atmosphere of emotionally overloaded and compulsive family ties that breed so many deep and abiding psychological problems." You are somewhat vague as to how the "collective family" will be established and how it will differ from the present state of affairs. Those who count themselves among your disciples will have to satisfy themselves with only a few general indications of how the family will operate in your utopia:

> There are deep sexual and emotional bonds between lovers, and between parents and children that must also be accommodated within a collective family. In that sense the collective family doesn't abolish the nuclear family but transcends it in a dialectical sense, i.e. it preserves romantic love and parental love while doing away with the

repressive relationships and social alienation that make family life such a misery in bourgeois society.

For you, Comrade Brenner, the problems of the family are rooted essentially, not in social conditions, but in individual psychology. Your animus is directed not so much against the existing economic system, as it is against the family, which you are convinced generates out of itself intense misery. What you therefore demand of socialists is that they invent a different, ideal, relationship – the so-called "collective family" – and place it in their program. This requires a significant misrepresentation of the attitude taken by Marx and Engels to this issue.[20]

---

20 You claim that Marx and Engels "openly defied the stifling morality of the Victorian age by calling for the abolition of the family and denouncing marriage as legalized prostitution." Without directly quoting Marx and Engels, you suggest to a reader unfamiliar with their writings that they were for the dissolution of all family relations, the practice of universal free love, etc. This corresponds to the caricature of communism found in the most reactionary literature. As a matter of fact, Marx and Engels did not speak of the family as an ahistorical abstraction in the *Communist Manifesto*. Rather, they posed the following question: "On what foundation is the *present* family, the *bourgeois* family, based?" They answered:

> On capital, on private gain. In its completely developed form this family exists only among the bourgeoisie. But this state of things finds its complement in the practical absence of the family among the proletarians, and in public prostitution.
>
> The bourgeois family will vanish as a matter of course when its complement vanishes, and both will vanish with the vanishing of capital." [New York, 1988, p. 71. Emphasis added]

Similarly, Marx and Engels speak not of marriage in general, but of bourgeois marriage. Their treatment of this issue begins with a mocking dismissal of the bourgeois claim that it is the intention of communists to create a "community of women," i.e., to make women the property of a public harem. They reply:

The bourgeois sees in his wife a mere instrument of production. He hears that the instruments of production are to be exploited in common, and, naturally, can come to no other conclusion than that the lot of being common to all will likewise fall to the women.

He has not even a suspicion that the real point aimed at is to do away with the status of women as mere instruments of production.

For the rest, nothing is more ridiculous than the virtuous indignation of our bourgeois at the community of women which, they pretend, is to be openly and officially established by the Communists. The Communists have no need to introduce community of women; it has existed almost from time immemorial.

Bourgeois marriage is in reality a system of wives in common and thus, at most, what the Communists might possibly be reproached with, is that they desire to introduce, in substitution for a hypocritically concealed, an openly legalized community of women. For the rest, it is self-evident that the abolition of the present system of production must bring with it the abolition of the community of women springing from that system, i.e., of prostitution both public and private." [ibid. p. 72]

In another essay, entitled *Principles of Communism* and which was written almost simultaneously with the *Communist Manifesto*, Engels offered the following reply to the question, "What influence will the communist order of society have on the family?"

It will make the relation between the sexes a purely private relation which concerns only the persons involved, and in which society has no call to interfere. It is able to do this because it abolishes private property and educates children communally, thus destroying the twin foundations of hitherto existing marriage – the dependence through private property of the wife upon the husband and of the children upon the parents. Here also is the answer to the outcry of moralizing philistines against the communist community of women. Community of women is a relationship that belongs altogether to bourgeois society and is completely realized today in prostitution. But prostitution is rooted in private property and falls with it. Thus instead of introducing the community of women,

For all your visionary pretensions, you seem singularly un-interested and ill-informed about the realities of life for most working class families. Fixated on the psychological and sexual dimension of the family trauma, you have remarkably little to say about the practical aspects of the problems confronting most working class families.[21] A reference to universal access to quality day care is thrown in as an aside. You give the impression of believing that there is relatively little that a socialist revolution can do, in terms of practical measures, which will significantly improve the conditions of working class families, aside from waging a propaganda campaign against various forms of social backwardness. "The nub of the issue is that the problems of the family," you write, "will not automatically disappear once socialism has arrived."

Whoever imagined that anything would happen automatically? The socialist revolution is not the same as launching an auto-install program on one's computer (which, as it so happens, is usually a process fraught with unforeseen difficulties). But this sort of remark, so typical of philistines, is intended to denigrate the basic perspective of socialism – that the key to the alleviation of all forms of human suffering lies in overthrowing the existing capitalistic property relations upon which contemporary society is based. The solution to the great problem posed by private ownership of the means of production will clear the way for the gradual solution of many other important problems of the human condition.

---

communist organization puts an end to it. [*Marx-Engels Collected Works*, Volume 6 (New York, 1976), p. 354]

21 There is no indication in your document that you have considered the urgent needs of families that live outside the wealthiest capitalist countries.

No, not all problems of inter-familial relationships will be solved in the first year of socialism, or even, perhaps, in its first century. No one can reasonably assume that under socialism all marriages or unions between conjugal partners will be happy or that all children will be satisfied with their parents or vice-versa. However, what we certainly can assume is that the major material causes of a great deal of present family hardship and misery will be alleviated fairly rapidly by a revolutionary reorganization of the economic structure of society along socialist lines.

A modern socialist program must address itself practically to the problems of men, women and children as they manifest themselves concretely in the first decade of the 21st century. Your reference to freeing women "from domestic servitude" appears somewhat quaint at a time when the overwhelming majority of mothers hold jobs outside their homes. You apparently have not noticed that the percentage of households corresponding to the "Father Knows Best" two-parent model is a fraction of what it was when that sitcom aired in the 1950s. And, we might add, the image of the authoritarian *paterfamilias* bears little relation to contemporary reality – especially that of working class fathers who find themselves in the clutches of that system of legal torture known as the "Friend of Court" (which can order the deduction of as much as half his weekly wage to cover child-support expenses). Working class families are beset by financial difficulties from which they can find no escape. The vast complexity of social life and the pressure it places upon families requires not the invention of a new family form, but rather shifting the weight of the burdens that now fall more or less entirely upon individuals to society as a whole.

But the significance of your discussion of the family lies not in the demands that you advance, but rather in the light you, Comrade Brenner, unwittingly shed on the wholly idealist outlook and method of contemporary neo-utopianism. You stress repeatedly that the family is a bulwark of social backwardness. But, as always, you locate the source of this backwardness not in the economic organization of society, but in individual psychology, specifically in "the repressed feelings in the unconscious" which persist in a human being's "congealed, unexamined past." You oppose the view that changes in the economic organization and structure of society will prove decisive in overcoming backwardness, which "will persist and perpetuate itself." An intervention of a different sort will be required: *"The content of that intervention is what this discussion is all about – the fight against sexual oppression and the socialist transformation of the family, since the only way to address problems at the root of human personality is to change the way human beings are brought up."* [Emphasis added]

The chasm between your perspective and that of the revolutionary socialist movement could not be stated more explicitly. Were your proposals and perspective to be adopted, the result would be the dissolution of the SEP, the ICFI and the Trotskyist movement. There would be no need for an international party whose aim is the revolutionary-strategic orientation of the international working class, based on the development of its conscious understanding of the objective laws governing the entire socio-economic system. The ICFI would be replaced by an organization focused on psychotherapy, examining the "repressed feelings in the unconscious" of its members and supporters, and addressing the sexual anxieties that you believe are embedded in the family structure.

We will return somewhat later to the very disturbing and reactionary implications of this deeply disoriented perspective. But first it is necessary to take note of the glaring contradiction in your argument. If, as you state, the vanquishing of social backwardness requires nothing less than a massive program of psychological rehabilitation, personality reconstruction, and the transformation of the family, how can the consciousness of

the masses ever be raised to the point where the revolution itself – upon which this unprecedented project of societal reengi-
neering depends – is even possible? In a society that consists of
people who are, according to you, Comrade Brenner, psycholog-
ically damaged as a result of their upbringing, how can socialism
become a mass movement? You cannot resolve this contradiction. Instead, you deepen it by reproducing the ahistorical conceptions of the old utopians. You assert, as did the old utopians,
that "the only way to address problems at the root of human
personality is to change the way human beings are brought up."
In other words, we must provide them with a different type of
family. But since this cannot be done, for obvious reasons, before the social revolution, it means that this conquest of power
must depend on the actions of people as they exist now – which
would seem to rule out a revolution. Yet, if, by some miracle, all
these damaged humans still manage to overthrow capitalism, it
will then be necessary to repair and reeducate them. Your conviction that the running of society must be left "for a considerable period of time" in the hands of specially trained socialists,
pre-indoctrinated with the prescribed consciousness, follows
logically from your idealist schema.[22]

---

22 The idea that the transformation of society depends upon changing human personality (i.e., human nature), which, in turn, depends upon
changing their upbringing, is the very conception that led the utopians
and their followers to organize their own sectarian societies, in which
the education of the youth would proceed in accordance with principles
laid down by the official educators. But these experiments, which all led
eventually to dead ends, were based on a fundamentally false conception
of social development. Marx subjected this utopian illusion to trenchant
criticism in the third of his *Theses on Feuerbach*:

> The [mechanical] materialist doctrine that men are product of
> circumstances and upbringing, and that, therefore, changed men
> are the product of other circumstances and changed upbringing,
> forgets that it is men who change circumstances and that the edu-

17. Bernstein, science and utopianism

In both your document, Comrade Brenner, and your joint letter, you repeatedly claim that the opposition to utopianism in the era of the Second International was largely a product of the growth of opportunism. "'Science' in the prewar Second International," you write, "was not just a disinterested development of theory (as North seems to believe); it was increasingly an *alibi* for absconding from revolutionary responsibilities, which 'objective conditions' would supposedly take care of. Hence the need to turn utopianism into a virtual taboo, because it threatened, not science but rather this objectivism. In the actual development of Marxism, however, scientific socialism was a dialectical 'aufheben' of its utopian predecessors, and utopia and science were not a rigid dichotomy but a *unity of opposites*, which is readily apparent in such canonical works as *Critique of the Gotha Program* or *State and Revolution*, to say nothing of a little gem like Paul Lafargue's *The Right to be Lazy*."

This account of the origins of anti-utopianism, buttressed by pseudo-dialectical bilingual phrasemongering[23], is essentially

---

cator must himself be educated. Hence, this doctrine is bound to divide society into two parts, one of which is superior to society (in Robert Owen for example).

The coincidence of the changing of circumstances and of human activity can be conceived and rationally understood only as revolutionary practice. [*Marx-Engels Collected Works*, Volume 5, p. 7]

23   The manner in which you employ Hegelian phraseology is sophistry of the purest water. In place of a real explanation of the relationship between utopianism and Marxism, you resort to terms such as aufheben and "unity of opposites.". This is simply a means of saying nothing, and making it appear profound. An example of the misuse to which pseudo-dialectical phraseology lends itself is shown in your invocation of Marx's *Critique of the Gotha Program* and Lenin's *State and Revolution*. These works, you say, demonstrate that utopianism and Marxism are a

"unity of opposites." What precisely does this mean? There is nothing utopian about either of these works (or even, except for certain stylistic devices that draw upon the literary tradition of Fourier and Proudhon, about Lafargue's *The Right to be Lazy*, which is, at any rate, a rather minor work).

Marx's *Critique* was written for the express purpose of demarcating his own scientific conceptions from all traces of the type of petty-bourgeois eclecticism and utopianism that characterized the conceptions of the Lassalleans. For example, Marx subjected the Lassallean's pledge of a "fair distribution" of the "proceeds of labor" to a withering criticism, insisting, in opposition to all utopian illusions, that "Right can never be higher than the economic structure of society and its cultural development which this determines." In justifying his severe attitude to various imprecise and/or incorrect formulations, Marx wrote that this stance was necessary "to show what a crime it is to attempt, on the one hand, to force on our Party again, as dogmas, ideas which in a certain period had some meaning but have now become obsolete verbal rubbish, while again perverting, on the other, the realistic outlook, which it cost so much effort to instill into the Party but which has now taken root in it, by means of ideological, legal and other trash so common among the Democrats and French Socialists." [*Marx Engels Collected Works*, Volume 24 (London, 1989), p. 87]

Lenin's *State and Revolution* elaborates a theory of the state on the basis of a comprehensive review of the writings of Marx and Engels on the subject. As in all the great "canonical works" (your phrase, Comrades Steiner and Brenner, not mine), Lenin counterposes explicitly and directly the scientific attitude of Marx to utopianism. As Lenin explains in one important and oft-quoted passage:

> There is no trace of utopianism in Marx, in the sense that he made up or invented a "new" society. No, he studied the *birth* of a new society *out of* the old, and the forms of the transition from the latter to the former. …
>
> We are not utopians. We do not "dream" of dispensing *at once* with all administrations, with all subordination. These anarchist dreams, based upon incomprehension of the tasks of the proletarian dictatorship, are totally alien to Marxism, and, as a matter of fact, serve only to postpone the socialist revolution until people are different. *No, we want the socialist revolution with people as they are now* [em-

false. Bernstein was not an enemy of utopianism. Bernstein argued against the conception that the socialist movement needed to legitimize its existence on the basis of science. He wrote: "There is no doubt that, although socialism as a practical proletarian movement has piled success upon success in many countries, formulating its position in ever clearer fashion, it experienced major setbacks as a scientific theory, losing its conceptual coherence and security in the cacophonous doubts and confusions of its representatives. Thus the legitimate question arises as to whether there exists an internal connection between socialism and science. To this concern regarding the possibility of a scientific socialism, I would like to add the question of whether a scientific socialism is needed at all." ["How is Scientific Socialism Possible," in *Selected Writings of Eduard Bernstein, 1900-1921* (New Jersey, 1996), p. 94]

Bernstein did not believe that it was necessary, or even desirable, that Marxism deny its links to utopianism, which he believed were necessarily present in a socialist movement. "However, whether one defines it as a condition, a theory, or a movement," he wrote, "socialism is always pervaded by an *idealistic* element that represents either the ideal itself or the movement toward such an ideal. Thus socialism is a piece of the *beyond* – obviously not beyond the planet we live on but beyond that of which we have a positive experience." [Ibid. p. 95]

Your claim that "It is Bernstein who pushes the counterposing of utopianism to science to its logical conclusion" is simply a misrepresentation of what the founder of modern revision-

---

phasis added], with people who cannot dispense with subordination, control and "foremen and accountants." [*Collected Works*, Volume 25 (Moscow, 1977), p. 430, emphasis in the original]

This latter passage is particularly apposite as a response to your claim that a socialist revolution requires the psychological reconditioning of the population.

ism wrote. He explained with great care that he did not employ the term utopian "as a euphemism for unrealistic dreams and fantasies." Such a use of the term, he protested, "would be a great injustice to those three great nineteenth-century utopian dreamers and forerunners of modern socialism…" [Ibid. p. 96] Far from presenting utopianism and Marxism as opposites, Bernstein argued that "If we investigate and compare the theories of these three utopians [Owen, Saint-Simon and Fourier] with Marx's theory, we shall find that Marx developed and emphasized the scientific element to a higher degree. But neither in the utopian writings nor in Marx's teachings is science *everything*. Of course, Marx draws narrower boundaries around the realm of will, imagination and inclination. But he does not fully erase it." [Ibid. p. 97]

Bernstein accused Engels of having exaggerated the chasm between the work of Marx and his utopian predecessors. "On the one hand he casts the utopians in an unfavorable light by overemphasizing the role of imagination in their writings, although they actually stressed discovery over invention. On the other hand he proclaims modern socialism freed from any form of invention. In my opinion socialism has never been, nor can it ever be, 'free of inventions and imaginings.'" [ibid. p. 97]

As these passages make clear, Bernstein recognized that the main challenge to his revisionist project stemmed not from utopianism but from the identification of socialism with science. In attacking the "objectivism" and "abstentionism" of the ICFI, it is you who are echoing the positions of Bernstein. Moreover, your repeated call for the revival of "socialist idealism" as the programmatic basis of a new socialist culture places you entirely within the camp of the revisionists on a key philosophical issue. Underlying the entire "Back to Kant" movement, which began in the late 1860s and ultimately played a major role in shaping the theoretical outlook of Bernstein and his supporters, was the conception that the struggle for socialism did not require scientific substantiation. The invocation of moral ideals – such as that which finds expression in Kant's second formulation of the categorical imperative ("Act in such a way that you always treat humanity, whether in your own person or in the person of any other, never simply as a means, but always at the same time as an end.") – could serve the struggle for socialism just as well as the Marxian conception of historical determinism. Indeed, a section of left academics in late 19th century Germany such as Karl Vorländer argued that the socialist movement ought to trace its philosophical lineage to Kant. In your own ill-informed haste to overthrow basic historical conceptions of Marxism, you have little concern for the theoretical roots and implications of your own arguments.

18. Neo-utopianism and
the demoralization of the petty-bourgeois left

Your document claims that my reference to neo-utopianism "is simply a straw man" that I have conjured up. You assert that I quoted from only one work, Vincent Geoghegan's *Utopianism and Marxism*, to substantiate my claim that this tendency exists, and that it represents a form of contemporary political pessimism. Actually, I also cited the *Socialist Register* for the year 2000, which is entitled *Necessary and Unnecessary Utopias*. However, I should have been more generous in my citations of this latter work, a defect that is easily remedied. Permit me to quote from the preface:

> The theme of this volume of the *Socialist Register* was first conceived in 1995 with the following general question in mind: as we approach the end of the millennium, what is to succeed the first great socialist project that was conceived in Western Europe in the nineteenth century,

and variously implemented in the twentieth? We had no illusion that an answer to this question would be found by cudgeling the brains of however large a number of left-wing intellectuals. But we did think that the time had come to renew the left's vision and spirit and that the *Register* could hope to contribute something useful for this purpose. We wanted to break with the legacy of a certain kind of Marxist thinking which rejected utopian thought as "unscientific" just because it was utopian, ignoring the fact that sustained political struggle is impossible without the hope of a better society that we can, in principle and in outline, imagine. And we particularly felt that, in the face of the collapse of communism, as well as the rejection by 'third way' social democracy of any identification with the socialist project, there was now, especially in the context of the growing crisis of the neo-liberal restoration, an opening as well as a need for imaginative thought." (Suffolk, 1999), p. vii

The clear connection between neo-utopianism and the demoralization prevailing among a layer of intellectuals, socialists and ex-radicals is established in the first contribution to this volume, which is entitled, "Transcending Pessimism: Rekindling Socialist Imagination." Written by Leo Panitch and Sam Gindin, many of the themes present in Brenner's essay are anticipated in this chapter – including the invocation of the work of Ernst Bloch, from whom you, Comrade Brenner obtained the title of your tract on utopianism (*To Know A Thing Is To Know Its End*)[24] Your own work is clear-

---

24 In his *The Principle of Hope*, Bloch wrote:

"The true genesis is not at the beginning, but at the end." It is simply not possible, within the framework of this document, to deal in depth

with the neo-utopian theories of Ernst Bloch (1885-1977). According to his biographer, Wayne Hudson, important influences in the development of Bloch's thought included Schopenhauer, Nietzsche, Kierkegaard, Dostoevsky, Brentano, Meinong, Vaihinger, Hermann Cohen, Rudolf Steiner, Georges Sorel, and Max Weber. The eclectic amalgamation of these diverse and generally reactionary influences, to which he added heavy doses of Jewish cabbalistic mysticism, constituted the "Marxism" of Ernst Bloch. Not surprisingly, Bloch was critical of the emphasis placed by Marx and Engels on economics, and of "their neglect of the secret transcendental elements in socialism." [*The Marxist Philosophy of Ernst Bloch* (New York, 1972), p. 33.] Hudson writes that Bloch believed that "Marxism, as Marx and Engels left it, was one-sided and lacked many of the elements necessary for the implementation of its project. Morality and love had not been given their proper place in the revolutionary struggle ... the Marxist conception of a heaven on earth was inadequate. Instead, it was necessary to take account of man's primal religious desire and to formulate a concept adequate to its intention. There had been too great a progress from utopia to science in Marxism, Bloch implied." [ibid., p. 33] Advocating a reconciliation with religion, Bloch argued (according to Hudson) that Marxism "needed to speak to people about their situation in language they could understand: to develop a propaganda which related to the ideology in their heads, instead of superstitiously relying on correct theoretical analysis to win a path for truth in the world." [ibid., p. 45]

Bloch remained throughout the 1930s a passionate supporter of Stalin, whom he regarded highly as a theoretician. Bloch enthusiastically supported the death sentences handed down at the Moscow trials. "Indeed," writes Hudson, "he prided himself on his ability to accept a degree of moral evil and the 'unmistakable smell of blood' as evidence of his political maturity ... He idealized the reality of Stalinist murder, and avoided the moral dilemma by accepting violence and 'red terror' in a context in which the fundamental good intentions of the revolutionary forces and their commitment to moral values as teleological ends could not be doubted." [ibid., p. 46] Later, in 1953, while living in the Stalinist German Democratic Republic, he issued no protest against the brutal suppression of the working class rebellion against the hated regime of Walter Ulbricht.

ly influenced by this chapter. Therefore, it is somewhat odd that you should deny that contemporary utopianism is a response to pessimism, because, as Panitch and Gindin point out, Bloch's own original work was motivated precisely by the effort to counter the pessimism generated by the catastrophes of the 1930s. As they note, "Bloch's response was to try to revive the idea of utopia. He insisted that even in a world where socialist politics are marginalized, we can still discover, if only in daydreams, the indestructible human desire for happiness and harmony, a yearning which consistently runs up against economic competition, private property and the bureaucratic state." [ibid. p. 2]

Panitch and Gindin make no secret of their own belief that Marxism is based on an unrealistic and exaggerated estimate of the revolutionary potential of the working class, writing that "it must be said that the historical optimism in Marx that inspired generations of socialists came with an underestimation of the scale and scope of the utopian dream and the capitalism-created agency honoured – or saddled – with carrying it out: the working class. Between Marx's broad historically-inspired vision of revolution/transformation and his detailed critique of political economy, there was an analytical and strategic gap – unbridgeable without addressing the problematic of working-class capacities – which later Marxists sometimes addressed, but never overcame. ... Every progressive social movement must, sooner or later, confront the inescapable fact that capitalism cripples our capacities, stunts our dreams, and incorporates our politics." [ibid. p. 5]

Comrades Steiner and Brenner: it is your right to oppose and criticize the International Committee, but don't take us

---

This is the man, Comrade Brenner, from whom you believe the International Committee has much to learn, and whose theoretical example you invoked in the title of your document on utopia!

for fools. We are quite familiar with the literature that is cir-
culating in petty-bourgeois political and academic circles, and
are able to identify the sources with which you are working. So
please don't argue that neo-utopianism – and the pessimism
from which it is derived – is a "straw man" that we created to
counter your brilliant original ideas. You are not deceiving us.
Rather, you are deceiving yourselves.

You go on to complain of references in my first lecture to
Geoghegan's *Utopianism and Marxism*, which you claim "is a
hatchet-job with quotes ripped out of context for the purpose
of proving that Geoghegan (and hence 'neo-Utopianism') ad-
vocate a left-version of Nazi-style mythmaking. But this again
is nonsense," you continue, "as is apparent to anyone who reads
the book. The point that Geoghegan was making in the quote
cited by North was that the Nazis were far more effective in
their appeals to mass psychology than the German left."[25]

The quotes are not ripped out of context. On the contrary, more extensive citations from Geoghegan would have
reinforced my assessment of his book as a work that attacks
Marxism for having underestimated the force and significance
of the irrational in the motivation of human behavior. In my
reference to Geoghegan, I stated that he "criticizes Marx and
Engels for 'having failed to develop a psychology. They left a
very poor legacy on the complexities of human motivation and
most of their immediate successors felt little need to overcome
this deficiency.'"

Let us place the quote in context by citing the entire paragraph from which it was "ripped." Geoghegan writes:

---

25 By this point, it should be fairly obvious to all objective readers
that you were well aware that my lectures last summer provided a reply
to your earlier documents. And, I might add, that your present document is an attempt to answer the critique of your views that were presented in the course of those lectures.

There has always been what one might term a rationalistic current in Marxism. It works with an Enlightenment model of the individual and its principal distinction is between knowledge and ignorance. This is its key to the central paradox of capitalism: that people put up with conditions not in their own interests. The ignorance which is false consciousness and alienation manifests itself in a variety of irrational beliefs and behaviors. However, once people break through this cocoon of illusion they will cease to behave in such a bizarre fashion. This is the spirit of Pottier's 'Internationale': "Arise! ye starvelings from your slumbers/ Arise ye criminals of want/ For reason in revolt now thunders/ And at last ends the age of cant." Such a view tends to privilege the bearers of knowledge: those who have emerged from the shadowy world of Plato's cave and have seen the light of truth. There was a strong dose of this type of rationalism in much of the Marxism of the Second International and it helped fuel the obsession with science. Part of the reason, which itself was part of the problem, was that Marx and Engels *failed to develop a psychology. They left a very poor legacy on the complexities of human motivation and most of their immediate successors felt little need to overcome this deficiency.* A simple concept of the individual coexisted with simplistic social strategies." [London and New York, 1987, pp. 67-68. Italicized words indicate those directly quoted in my lecture last August.]

The entire paragraph in no way contradicts my summary of Geoghegan's argument. Rather than complaining that I have misquoted the author, you should explain why, and by what process, you have come to agree with his views. I have already noted your ambivalent attitude to the Enlightenment. The passage cited above reveals not only the parentage of your earlier objection to my "uncritical defense of the Enlightenment"; it also makes clear that your embrace of neo-utopianism has placed you in extremely unhealthy ideological and political company.[26]

---

26 It is unfortunate that you have failed to investigate the various sources from which Geoghegan has drawn inspiration. All the ideas advanced in this one paragraph that you vehemently defend against my criticisms – that Marxism is excessively rationalistic, that it is mistaken in its conviction that workers will embrace socialism if they acquire knowledge of their objective class interests, that it lacks an adequate knowledge of human psychology, and that it is based on a false theory of historical motivation – were anticipated and developed in considerable detail some 80 years ago by Hendrik de Man, in a book entitled *The Psychology of Socialism*. De Man, a Belgian socialist who taught in the 1920s at the University of Frankfurt, broke from Marxism in the aftermath of the First World War. The mass slaughter of 1914-1918, which he witnessed as a soldier, led de Man to move "from the outlook of economic determinism, which forms the basis of Marxist socialism, to the standpoint of a philosophy wherein the main significance is allotted to the individual human being as a subject to psychological reactions." [Originally published in 1926 as *Zur Psychologie des Sozialismus*. English edition cited here was published by Henry Holt and Company, New York, 1972. This passage appears on page 13.]

De Man asserted that the basic flaw of Marxism was its belief that human behavior was subject to rational explanation, and that socialism arose as a response within the working class to its class interests. Marxism, he wrote, "obstinately" ignores the "multiplicity of socialist motivation, refuses to see the complicated nature of the issues. Otherwise the Marxists would lose their faith in the necessary connexion between class interests and ways of thinking." [ibid., p. 28]

The Psychology of Socialism was immensely influential within German academic circles in the 1920s, especially in the city where the Frankfurt School was taking shape under the leadership of Friedrich Pollack and Max Horkheimer. Though de Man's thoroughgoing repudiation of Marxism was not acceptable to the founders of the Frankfurt School, his attempt to supplant historical materialism with psychology anticipated trends that were to become increasingly pronounced among Horkheimer's colleagues. As for de Man, he achieved considerable fame

19. What did Daniel Guerin really write?

You assert repeatedly that the International Committee fails to understand the importance of and ignores "human factors" that are critical to the struggle for socialism. We are making the same error, you suggest, as that made by the Stalinists and Social Democrats prior to Hitler's victory in 1933, who "in the name of a spurious 'materialism' were contemptuous of the role of political idealism in mobilizing mass support." In support of this argument, you refer to *Fascism and Big Business*, the well-known work of Daniel Guerin, a Trotskyist in the 1930s. You quote precisely one passage from this 318-page book: "The degenerated Marxists believe it is very 'Marxist' and 'materialist' to disdain the human factors. They accumulate figures, statistics and percentages; they study with great accuracy the profound causes of social phenomena. But by failing to study with the same care the way in which the causes *are reflected in the consciousness of men*, and failing to penetrate the soul of man, they miss the *living reality* of these phenomena."

Commenting on this passage, you state that "This was exactly what Reich and Fromm were saying in the Thirties and what Geoghegan was reprising in the remarks North found so outrageous." Thus, the conclusion that you want the reader

---

in the 1930s when he wrote, under the "inspiration" of the ephemeral economic successes of Hitler's regime, his *Plan du Travail*. De Man envisaged an alliance of the working class and middle class on the basis of a national economic program of state-regulated capitalism. After the Nazis invaded Belgium, where he had been a "socialist" government minister, de Man became a fascist collaborator. At the end of the war, de Man fled Belgium, which then tried him for treason *in absentia*. He died in Switzerland in 1953. His life is an extreme but by no means unique example of the erratic biographical trajectory of those who have sought to separate socialism from historical materialism. It is a reactionary project with politically dangerous consequences.

to draw is that Guerin believed that too great an emphasis on science and a materialist explanation of objective conditions, and the absence among Marxists of a sufficient understanding of psychology, contributed significantly to the Nazi victory. As Guerin was a well-known Trotskyist in the 1930s, you would have your readers believe that this was also the view of Leon Trotsky.

But, once again, your presentation of a quotation is misleading and dishonest. Three sentences are cited in support of *your* arguments, which are, as we shall see, very different from those of Guerin. Who are the "degenerated Marxists" of whom he is writing? What is the "spurious materialism" that Guerin condemns?

Let us repeat a procedure that we have employed several times in this document. We will go back to the author's actual text and place your citation in the appropriate context. The chapter from which you have obtained the citation is entitled "Fascist Mysticism," which offers a valuable account of the propaganda and agitation techniques employed by the fascists to delude and deceive the masses. Guerin points out that the appeals made by the fascists to the emotions and blind faith of potential followers are determined by the class interests they serve. "A party supported by the subsidies of the propertied classes, with the secret aim of defending the privileges of property owners, is not interested in appealing to the intelligence of its recruits; or rather, it considers it prudent not to appeal to their understanding until they have been thoroughly bewitched." [*Fascism and Big Business* (New York, 1973), p. 63]

Guerin goes on to explain that the appeal to blind faith is facilitated by the fact that fascism "is fortunate enough to address its appeal to the miserable and discontented." He observes that "It is a psychological phenomenon, as old as the world, that suffering predisposes to mysticism. When man suffers, he renounces reason, ceases to demand logical remedies for his ills, and no longer has the courage to try to save himself. He expects a miracle and he calls for a savior, whom he is ready to follow, for whom he is ready to sacrifice himself.

"Finally, fascism has the advantage – if we may say so – over socialism in that it despises the masses. It does not hesitate to conquer them through their weaknesses." [ibid. pp. 63-64]

One has only to read this passage to recognize immediately how fundamentally incompatible Guerin's views are with those of Geoghegan, whose work you so warmly endorse. Guerin sees in the irrationalism of the fascist appeal an expression of its reactionary objectives, not a psychological model to be learned from, let alone emulated.

Several pages later, after completing his analysis of fascist propaganda and mass mobilization techniques, Guerin poses the critical question: *"What has the labor movement done to combat fascist 'mysticism?'"* The reasons that Guerin gives for the labor movement's failure to develop effective methods bear no resemblance to the position advanced by Geoghegan. First of all, Guerin makes clear that certain problems that socialists confront in the area of mass agitation flow from the "very nature" of socialism. He explains that "Socialism is less a religion than a scientific conception. Therefore it appeals more to intelligence and reason than to the senses and imagination. Socialism does not impose a faith to be accepted without discussion; it presents a rational criticism of the capitalist system and requires of everybody, before his adherence, a personal effort of reason and judgment. It appeals more to the brain than to the eye or the nerves; it seeks to convince the reader or listener calmly, not to seize him, move him, and hypnotize him." [ibid. p. 73]

Guerin allows that socialism's propaganda techniques need "to be rejuvenated and modernized," in order to "place itself more within the reach of the masses, and to speak to them in clear and direct language that they will understand." However, Guerin immediately qualifies this suggestion with the warning that socialism "cannot, *on pain of self-betrayal*, appeal like fascism to the lower instincts of crowds. Unlike fascism, *it does not despise the masses*, but respects them. It wants them to be better than they are, to be the image of the conscious proletariat from which socialism emanates. It strives, not to lower, but to raise their intellectual and moral level." [ibid. pp. 73-74, emphasis in the original]

Comrades Steiner and Brenner, to your own shame you did not quote these very wonderful and beautiful words because you understand very well that they speak in defense of the Marxist confidence in the power of reason, and uphold the view that the victory of socialism requires the raising of political consciousness, not the psychological manipulation of the unconscious. Nowhere in Guerin's book – whose central purpose, let us not forget, was to expose the objective economic and political links between fascism and the ruling elite (that is, to provide a scientific insight into the political phenomenon of fascism) – is there any suggestion that the problem with Marxism is its "obsession with science."

Why, then, was socialism unable to counter effectively the agitation of the fascists? In what way did the socialist movement "degenerate?" Guerin's answer is that the socialist movement became politically opportunist. "It came to believe," he writes, "that immediate advantages, as well as the 'paradise on earth,' could be achieved without struggle and sacrifice, by the vulgar practice of 'class collaboration.'" [ibid. p. 74] Guerin writes with scorn of the labor bureaucrats, describing them memorably as "conservative and routine-minded, implanted in the existing order, well fed and complacent high priests, who ruled in buildings paid for by workers' pennies and called 'people's houses.' To win a legislative seat or find a soft berth in a union office had become the rule of life for the leaders of this degenerate socialism. They no longer believed, they enjoyed. And they wanted troops in their own image, troops without ideals, attracted only by material advantages." [ibid. p. 75]

The degeneration of which Guerin writes was rooted not in the failure and inadequacies of Marxism, but in the opportunism of the labor bureaucracy. Then, in the paragraph that immediately precedes the passage you cite, Guerin explains the manner in which opportunism undermined the Marxist method.

> At the same time, in the field of doctrine, socialism distorted one of its essential conceptions, "historical materialism." The first Marxian socialists were *materialists* in the sense that, according to them, "the means of production in economic life condition in general the processes of social, political and intellectual life." Unlike the "idealists," for whom the profoundest motive force in history is an already existing *idea* of justice and right which humanity bears in itself and which it achieves gradually through centuries, those early socialists thought that the relations of production, the economic relations of men with each other, play a preponderant role in history. But if they stressed the economic base, too often neglected before them, they in no way disdained the juridical, political, religious, artistic, and philosophical 'superstructure.' That was conditioned, they believed, by the base, but the superstructure had its own value none the less, and was an integral part of history. [ibid. p. 75, emphasis in the original]

Finally, but in its proper context, following a defense and restatement of the Marxist materialist conception of history, we come to the passage that you cited and which we will quote again in the interest of clarity:

The degenerated Marxists believe it is very "Marxist" and "materialist" to disdain the human factors. They accumulate figures, statistics and percentages; they study with great accuracy the profound causes of social phenomena. But by failing to study with the same care the way in which the causes are *reflected in the consciousness of men*, and failing to penetrate the soul of man, they miss the *living reality* of these phenomena.

Now we can properly understand the point that Guerin is making. True to its own opportunism, the degenerate bureaucracy practiced a vulgar and mechanical caricature of Marxism – incapable of understanding the myriad forms through which the increasingly desperate situation confronting capitalist society found conscious expression in politics and mass consciousness. Tied to the fleshpots of the Weimar democracy, the corrupted socialist movement could not find a way to appeal to the masses. The problem lay not in Marxism, in historical materialism, but in the opportunist repudiation of Marxism's revolutionary perspective and commitment to struggle.

Guerin concludes his analysis by warning that "Thousands and thousands of men, women, and adolescents who are burning to give themselves, will never be attracted to a socialism reduced to the most opportunistic parliamentarism and vulgar trade unionism. Socialism can regain its attractive force only by saying to the masses that to win the 'paradise on earth,' its supreme goal requires great struggles and sacrifices."

In bringing our review of Guerin's book to a conclusion, it should be noted that in his preface to the 1965 French edition, the author acknowledged that "the writings of Leon Trotsky on Germany and France served as a guide. They helped me understand the complex problem of the middle classes, who wavered between the proletariat and the bourgeoisie, and who were propelled by the economic crisis on the one hand, and the default of the working class on the other, towards the gangsters of the ultraright." [ibid. p. 17]

20. Wilhelm Reich's conception of socialist consciousness

In the course of your defense of Geoghegan, you refer favorably to the work of Wilhelm Reich. In this case, I cannot object to the connection that you make between the former and the latter. You are correct when you state that Geoghegan's assertion that the Nazis "were far more effective in their appeals to mass psychology than the German left" essentially repeated the arguments made by Wilhelm Reich in the 1930s. In agreement with Reich, you write that "political consciousness was a battleground that the left was ignoring with disastrous consequences," and that "Socialism could only triumph by winning over the allegiance of millions of workers and for that to happen the left had to find a way of engaging the hopes, fears and dreams of those millions."

The question that arises is how the development of "political" and "socialist" consciousness was understood by Wilhelm Reich. You have surprisingly little to say on this subject in your document, noting only in passing that Reich demonstrated "in practice" how a "renewed socialist idealism" could be developed "with the fascinating work he did in the early Thirties with German working class youth in the sex-pol movement." Aside from implying that this work holds great lessons for contemporary socialists, you fail to present either a summary of Reich's views or explain their enduring relevance. However, in a document entitled "Utopia and Revolution," which you, Comrade Steiner, wrote in 2004 and sent to Comrade Steve Long of the ICFI, you provided an indication of what you believe to be the crucial insight of Wilhelm Reich. Arguing in support of positions advanced by Herbert Marcuse in his *Eros and Civilization*, you explained that Marcuse "essentially makes the same point that Wilhelm Reich did in his *Mass Psychology of Fascism*, that if the Marxist movement does not find a way to channel repressed libidinal drives in a progressive direction, then fascism will utilize those same drives to bring us into an age of barbarism." You immediately added: "I could say a great deal more on this subject but I think I have made my point."

Indeed, you did. What you understand and mean by the struggle for "political" and "socialist" consciousness has absolutely nothing to do with Marxism. Much of what you write is based on the work of Wilhelm Reich, whose conceptions are fundamentally alien to historical materialism and the revolutionary Marxist tradition. Of course, Reich was a product of his time and culture, and there was a genuine element of tragedy in his life. He was, like so many others, a victim of the catastrophe that swept over the working class and socialist intellectuals in the 1930s and 1940s. His work and conceptions, which assumed an increasingly obsessive, disoriented and even politically right-wing character after his arrival in the United States, bore the ineradicable imprint of the massive defeat inflicted by fascism on the German and European working class during the 1930s. How can one not feel sympathy for the sad fate of this exiled European psychologist, torn from the Vienna and Berlin milieu in which his own intellectual development was rooted, whose explorations into the field of human sexuality aroused the ire of vindictive American authorities and landed him in the federal prison in Lewisburg, Pennsylvania, where he died in 1957 at the age of 60? His life deserves to be studied sympathetically and with respect. Fortunately, such an approach can be found in *Fury on Earth*, a biography written by Myron Sharaf.

But sympathy for the human and cultural tragedy of Wilhelm Reich does not extend to your efforts to dilute or replace Marxism and Trotskyism with Reichian "sex-politics." For that we have no patience whatsoever. The attempt to derive a strategy for socialism from Reich's sexual theories, particularly as they are presented in *The Mass Psychology of Fascism*, can only result in the worst forms of political disorientation. On what is certainly one of the most serious questions arising from the history of the socialist movement in the 20th century – that is, why the German working class was defeated by Hitler and the Nazis – the answers given by Reich are saturated with a morbid pessimism that is incompatible with a revolutionary perspective. His rooting of fascism in an innately and universally deranged human psychology has no basis in historical materialism. Moreover, the answers given by Reich not only lead to a false political perspective and program, they can only lead those who accept them away from revolutionary politics and socialism, a trajectory anticipated in Reich's own evolution.

In December 1933, Wilhelm Reich, having escaped to Denmark, wrote under the pseudonym of Ernst Parrell a pamphlet entitled *What Is Class Consciousness?* This relatively brief work summed up the conclusions he drew from the defeat of the German working class.

The most notable aspect of Reich's pamphlet is the cursory attention given to issues of program and perspective. Virtually nothing is said about the actual policies pursued by the Social Democrats and Stalinists, which demoralized and split the working class, and cleared the way for the Nazi victory. These were not questions of particular interest to Reich. The essential cause of the defeat of the working class was to be found, not in the craven opportunism of the Social Democrats or the ultra-left "Third Period" adventurism of the Communist Party, but rather in "the lack of an effective Marxian political psychology

… This deficiency on our part was of the greatest advantage to the class enemy, and became one of the most powerful weapons of fascism. While we were presenting the masses with grandiose historical analyses and economic arguments about the contradictions of imperialism, their innermost feelings were being kindled for Hitler." [London, 1971, p. 18]

In presenting his conception of class consciousness, Reich betrayed an attitude to the intellectual capacities of the working class that bordered on utter contempt. He considered it nothing less than absurd to believe that masses of workers would be receptive to questions such as "knowledge about the contradictions of the capitalist economic system, the terrific possibilities of socialist planning, the necessity of social revolution in order to accommodate the forms of appropriation to the form of production, and about the progressive and reactionary forces in history." These questions were of importance to party leaders, and formed elements of their more developed class consciousness. But class consciousness among the masses "is remote from such knowledge, and from wide perspectives; it is concerned with petty matters, banal everyday questions." Problems of international politics were quite necessarily the concern of political leaders. But the mass working class consciousness "is completely unconcerned by the quarrels of Russia and Japan, or England and America, and in the progress of the productive forces; it is oriented solely and exclusively by the reflections, expressions and effects of this objective process in a million different little everyday questions; it is therefore made up of concern about food, clothing, family relationships, the possibilities of sexual satisfaction in the narrowest sense, sexual pleasure and amusement in a broader sense, such as the cinema, theatre, fairground entertainments and dancing, also with the difficulties of bringing up children, furnishing the house, with the length and utilization of free time, etc. etc." [ibid. p. 22]

Therefore, the most critical task of Marxists must be to "find the connection with the petty, banal, primitive, simple everyday life and wishes of the *broadest* mass of the people in all the specificity of their situation in society." [ibid. p. 23]

Quite apart from the issues of sexuality upon which Reich placed such overriding emphasis, his attitude toward the development of socialist consciousness reflected the weight of social influences outside the great intellectual and cultural traditions of the Marxist movement. Reich's outlook expressed a particularly vulgar form of political opportunism that is often encountered among intellectuals whose conception of the working class is impressionistic, ahistorical and, one might add, steeped in the prejudices of their own middle-class and professional milieu. They do not perceive the proletariat as a historically rising class, the protagonist of a new and higher form of social organization. Rather, they see only an agglomeration of backward and ignorant individuals, rising hardly above the level of brute beasts, ignorant and indifferent to culture, and devoid of serious interests. What then, such intellectuals think, is the point of talking to workers about history, politics, economics and culture? It is necessary to get down to the lowest level possible, so that our ideas will be accessible to the masses. Curiously, such an attitude often goes hand in hand with a glorification of non-political trade unionism.

Why, one is compelled to ask, did the first, most powerful and politically advanced mass workers' party in history arise in Germany? This historical phenomenon is undoubtedly linked to the astonishing development of culture associated with the *Aufklärung* (Enlightenment). The history of the German mass socialist movement, which arose on the basis of the revolution in philosophical thought that began with Kant in the latter half of the 18th century, testified to the organic link between advanced theory and a powerful class-conscious workers movement. The legacy of Kant, Lessing, Hegel, Feuerbach,

Goethe, Schiller, Kleist, Mozart and Beethoven, interacting with the impact of the French Revolution, created an extraordinary cultural-intellectual environment that proved to be exceptionally favorable for the development of mass socialist consciousness in the new proletariat, which grew rapidly with the industrialization of Germany. Indeed, it was in the towering figure of Marx that the entire antecedent intellectual development of Germany found its concentrated expression.

Marx could not have written that philosophy is the head of the emancipation of humanity and the proletariat its heart if he had conceived of the working class in the manner of Reich. Nor would Engels have stated that "The German working-class movement is the heir to German classical philosophy." [*Marx-Engels Collected Works*, Volume 26 (Moscow, 1990), p. 398] The German Social Democracy, with its innumerable educational associations and projects, was not only a political but also a mighty cultural movement of the working class, spurred on by teachers who were imbued with a theoretically-grounded understanding of the historical mission of the working class. How could they possibly have pursued their revolutionary pedagogic work, tirelessly lecturing and writing, if they had believed that the German working class was indifferent to their efforts? One cannot possibly imagine Franz Mehring and Rosa Luxemburg writing of the proletariat in the manner of Reich.[27]

Reich's debased conception of class consciousness reflected not only his own social prejudices, but also the desperation

---

27 Permit me to point out that Comrade David Walsh addressed the issue of the cultural work of the socialist movement, not only in Germany but throughout Europe, in the very important lecture that he delivered at last summer's school ("Marxism, Art, and the Soviet Debate over 'Proletarian Culture'"). Unfortunately, your document makes no reference whatever to this lecture.

produced by a political catastrophe whose causes he did not understand. Political opportunism is not infrequently a by-product of desperation. One has the impression that Reich believed that he had discovered in sexual questions a means of obtaining access to mass consciousness without having to deal with complex political and theoretical issues that he considered incomprehensible to the working class. Young people, he believed, were particularly open to such an approach: "We cannot theoretically prove to the youth of all lands and continents the need for socialist revolution, but only develop it from the needs and contradictions of youth. In the center of those needs and contradictions stands the tremendous question of the sex life of young people." [*What Is Class Consciousness*, p. 30][28]

The blatantly opportunist and, one might add, rather naïve character of Reich's conviction that "sex-politics" provided a master key for obtaining access to the masses is illustrated in a lengthy passage in which he purported to show how socialists, intervening covertly in fascist gatherings, could win a hearing even from dedicated Nazis by cleverly initiating a dialogue about permissible forms of sexual activity.

> …If a logically thinking person had got up in a [Nazi] meeting and asked concretely where the difference lies between morality and prudishness, any Nazi official would have found himself in a very embarrassing situation. Thus, it is prudish to forbid women to go out

---

28 For all his frankness in addressing questions of sexuality, he was not above the prejudices of his time: "The more distinctly the natural heterosexual tendencies attain development, the more accessible the young person is to revolutionary ideas; the more strongly the homosexual need asserts itself in his psychic structure and the more restricted his consciousness of sexuality in general, the easier he is drawn to the right." [p. 28]

with young men, and not the moral excellence which National Socialism demands; so going out is permitted. But what if a young man kisses a woman? Is that moral? Or if he even wishes to have sexual relations with her? That surely comes under the enjoyment of life, doesn't it? Should the Nazi make further concessions at this point and even admit free love – which he is quite capable of doing – he would be further asked whether this, if openly permitted, would not compromise the consolidation of marriage and the family ...

After continuing his imaginary dialogue along these lines, Reich asserts:

> It must be admitted that tactics of this sort could bring about a lively public debate in an entirely unpolitical form which could be a hundred times more embarrassing for the Nazis than a thousand illegal leaflets, for the simple reason that the Nazis would be unconsciously making propaganda for us. There's no such thing as class consciousness? It's present in every nook and cranny of everyday life! You can't develop it or you'll get thrown into jail? Take up these questions which concern every Nazi most closely, those which the Right can never answer, and you can forget about the question of class consciousness. The role of the avantgarde during a period of illegality? We're not interested in the problem; it's the concrete substance of proletarian democracy that concerns us, and not the slogan of proletarian democracy which means nothing to nine people out of ten. [ibid. p. 35]

Convinced that revolutionary politics can be successful only when it learns "in content and form" to "express the primitive, unsophisticated feeling of the broad mass," Reich quite naturally concluded that the emphasis the Trotskyists placed on clarifying the issues that separated political tendencies was a waste of energy. Arguing directly against Trotsky's call for the formation of the Fourth International, Reich wrote that "The masses, however, understand nothing of the fine differences between individual revolutionary tendencies, and are uninterested in them." [ibid. p. 53]

The Mass Psychology of Fascism, in which Reich presented his explanation for the victory of the Nazis, is a work which gives expression to the deepest despair. The growth of fascism as a mass movement was not the product of political conditions but of the diseased state of the human psyche. He insisted that fascism should not be seen, in essence, as a political movement. Its political structure was merely the outer form of a more deeply rooted human phenomenon. Reich wrote:

> [M]y medical experiences with men and women of various classes, races, nations, religious beliefs, etc., taught me that "fascism" is only the organized political expression of the structure of the average man's character, a structure that is confined neither to certain races or nations nor to certain parties, but is general and international. Viewed with respect to man's character, *"fascism" is the basic emotional attitude of the suppressed man of our authoritarian machine civilization, and its mechanistic-mystical conception of life."* [*The Mass Psychology of Fascism* (New York, 1970), p. xiii]

Reich wrote that he had become convinced that "there is not a single individual who does not bear the elements of fascist feeling and thinking in his structure ... In its pure form fascism is the sum total of all the *irrational* reactions of the average human character." [ibid. p. xiv]

Marxist parties could not stop Hitler, Reich insisted, "because they tried to comprehend twentieth-century fascism, which was something completely new, with concepts belonging to the nineteenth century." [ibid. p. xxi] Marxism incorrectly attempted to analyze fascism within the context of the historical development of capitalism over the previous 200 years. But fascism "raised the basic question of *man's character, human mysticism* and *craving for authority,* which covered a *period of some four to six thousand years.* Here, too, vulgar Marxism sought to ram an elephant into a foxhole." [ibid. p. xxvi]

The state of mankind as diagnosed by Reich was all but hopeless.

> As bitter as it may be, the fact remains: It is the irresponsibleness of masses of people that lies at the basis of fascism of all countries, nations, and races, etc. Fascism is the result of man's distortion over thousands of years. ... That this situation was brought about by a social development which goes back thousands of years does not alter the fact itself. It is man himself who is responsible and not "historical developments." It was this shifting of the responsibility from living man to "historical developments" that caused the downfall of the socialist freedom movement. [ibid. p. 320]

For all the exotic and original elements of Reich's psychosexual account of mankind's descent into fascism, in essence his arguments were fundamentally in agreement with the view, widely held in demoralized left circles, that Hitler's victory was irrefutable proof of the organic incapacity of the working class to carry out a social revolution. As you might vaguely recall from your earlier studies, Comrades Steiner and Brenner, there existed numerous left groupings in the

1930s who expressed dissatisfaction with Trotsky's attribution of responsibility for the defeats of the working class to the false and treacherous policies of their political leaders in the Stalinist and Social Democratic parties. That explanation, Trotsky's left-centrist critics responded, was altogether inadequate. Yes, perhaps the leaders made mistakes and even consciously betrayed their followers. But why did the masses "allow" themselves to be betrayed? Did they not bear responsibility for what happened? Could they not have opposed their leaders? Is it not necessary to examine critically the masses themselves and identify those organic elements of their being, whether lodged in immutable characteristics of their social existence or in their psyche, which condition them to follow wrong leaders and accept their own defeat?

In answering such questions, which reflected an apologetic attitude toward the parties that presided over the political disasters suffered by the masses, Trotsky explained the relationship between the working class and its leadership. It is not true, Trotsky wrote, that people get the government – or that workers get the leaders – they deserve. Both governments and leaders emerge as the product of a complex process involving both the struggle between classes and internal conflicts among the heterogeneous elements of which the classes themselves are composed. The formation of the leadership of the working class is an immensely difficult and protracted historical process, reflected in the struggle of tendencies that may stretch over many decades. The emergence out of this process of an authoritative leadership, whose prestige among the masses has been acquired through long and difficult struggle, is a historical achievement. However, there remains the danger that the leadership, having acquired authority among the masses, may, over time, come under the pressure exerted by other classes and undergo an internal degeneration. Neither the fact of degeneration, let alone its degree, may be immediately apparent to the masses, who continue to retain their confidence in their traditional leaders. Especially under conditions of relative social tranquility – that is, precisely during those periods when placid daily routines foster tendencies toward opportunist adaptation – the natural tendency to extend trust beyond the point when it is merited politically is especially pronounced. The gap between the policies pursued by the old parties, and the changing requirements arising out of a rapidly shifting political situation goes unnoticed – until the crisis prepared by unseen socio-economic contradictions emerges in the form of a great historical shock. Trotsky explained:

> …The mightiest historical shocks are wars and revolutions. Precisely for this reason the working class is often caught unawares by war and revolution. But even in cases where the old leadership has revealed its internal corruption, the class cannot immediately improvise a new leadership, especially if it has not inherited from the previous period strong revolutionary cadres capable of utilizing the collapse of the old leading party. ["The Class, the Party, and the Leadership," in *The Spanish Revolution (1931-39)* (New York, 1973), p. 358]

Trotsky denounced all forms of political apologetics that seek to place on the working class responsibility for the mistakes and crimes of its leaders, fail to examine the role played in the political struggle by "such concrete factors as programs, parties, and personalities that were the organizers of defeat," and present the victory of fascism in Germany, Spain or Italy "as a necessary link in the chain of cosmic developments…" [ibid. p. 364] The only essential difference between Reich's explanation of the defeat of the German working class and that of the centrist tendencies criticized by Trotsky was that the "cosmic developments" that preordained fascism's triumph were, for Reich, of a sexual rather than a sociological-political character.

But let us now turn to the question of mass psychology, which cannot be ignored by revolutionaries. One can learn far more about the social psychology out of which German fascism emerged by reading Trotsky than by poring over the works of Reich. When was the last time, Comrades Steiner and Brenner, that you read Trotsky's brilliant essay, "What Is National Socialism"? Here, Trotsky depicted the social, economic and political conditions of post-World War I Germany that created the psychological conditions in which Hitler's barbaric movement could win millions of adherents from the middle classes:

> The postwar chaos hit the artisans, the peddlers, and the civil employees no less cruelly than the workers. The economic crisis in agriculture was ruining the peasantry. The decay in the middle strata did not mean that they were made into proletarians, inasmuch as the proletariat itself was casting out a gigantic army of chronically unemployed. The pauperization of the petty bourgeoisie, barely covered by ties and socks of artificial silk, eroded all official creeds and first of all the doctrine of democratic parliamentarism.
>
> The multiplicity of parties, the icy fever of elections, the interminable changes in ministries aggravated the social crisis by creating a kaleidoscope of barren political combinations. In the atmosphere brought to white heat by war, defeat, reparations, inflation, occupation of the Ruhr, crisis, need, and despair, the petty bourgeoisie rose up against all the old parties that had bamboozled it. The sharp grievances of small proprietors never out of bankruptcy, of their university sons without posts and clients, of their daughters without dowries and suitors, demanded order and an iron hand.
>
> The banner of National Socialism was raised by up-starts from the lower and middle commanding ranks of

the old army. Decorated with medals for distinguished service, commissioned and noncommissioned officers could not believe that their heroism and sufferings for the Fatherland had not only come to naught, but also gave them no special claims to gratitude. Hence their hatred of the revolution and the proletariat. At the same time, they did not want to reconcile themselves to being sent by the bankers, industrialists, and ministers back to the modest posts of bookkeepers, engineers, postal clerks, and schoolteachers. Hence their "socialism." At the Yser and under Verdun they had learned to risk themselves and others, and to speak the language of command, which powerfully overawed the petty bourgeois behind the lines. Thus these people became leaders.

At the start of his political career, Hitler stood out only because of his big temperament, a voice much louder than others, and an intellectual mediocrity much more self-assured. He did not bring into the movement any ready-made program, if one disregards the insulted soldier's thirst for vengeance. Hitler began with grievances and complaints about the Versailles terms, the high cost of living, the lack of respect for a meritorious noncommissioned officer, and the plots of bankers and journalists of the Mosaic persuasion. There were in the country plenty of ruined and drowning people with scars and fresh bruises. They all wanted to thump with their fists on the table. This Hitler could do better than others. True, he knew not how to cure the evil. But his harangues resounded, now like commands and now like prayers addressed to inexorable fate. Doomed classes, like those fatally ill, never tire of making variations on their plaints nor of listening to consolations. Hitler's speeches were all attuned to this pitch. Sentimental formlessness, absence of disciplined thought, ignorance along with gaudy erudition – all these minuses turned into pluses. They supplied him with the possibility of uniting all types of dissatisfaction into the beggar's bowl of National Socialism, and of leading the mass in the direction it pushed him. In the mind of the agitator was preserved, from among his early improvisations, whatever had met with approbation. His political thoughts were the fruits of oratorical acoustics. That is how the selection of slogans went on. That is how the program was consolidated. That is how the "leader" took shape out of the raw material. ...

The immense poverty of National Socialist philosophy did not, of course, hinder the academic sciences from entering Hitler's wake with all sails unfurled, once his victory was sufficiently plain. For the majority of the professorial rabble, the years of the Weimar regime were periods of riot and alarm. Historians, economists, jurists, and philosophers were lost in guesswork as to which of the contending criteria of truth was right, that is, which of the camps would turn out in the end the master of the situation. The fascist dictatorship eliminates the doubts of the Fausts and the vacillations of the Hamlets of the university rostrums. Coming out of the twilight of parliamentary relativity, knowledge once again enters into the kingdom of absolutes. Einstein has been obliged to pitch his tent outside the boundaries of Germany. [Leon Trotsky, *The Struggle Against Fascism in Germany* (New York, 1971), pp. 462-67]

In these few paragraphs, Trotsky explained, with incomparable brilliance, the social and political origins of the madness of German fascism, the relationship between objective socio-economic processes and the bizarre forms of their reflections in the psyche of the German middle class. It is true that

Trotsky was a politician and writer of genius. But his genius was nourished by Marxism, and he demonstrated what can be achieved on the basis of historical materialist analysis. The insight that he provides is not merely of literary and historical interest, but retains enduring relevance as an analysis of the political instability of petty bourgeois layers in society and the underlying objective causes of their susceptibility to fascistic propaganda. Trotsky demystifies the fascist phenomenon. And, by making fascism comprehensible, he indicates the political means by which it can be combated and defeated.

Can the same be said of the analysis of Wilhelm Reich, who informed us that

> …The man whose genitals are weakened, whose sexual structure is full of contradictions must continually remind himself to control his sexuality, to preserve his sexual dignity, to be brave in the face of temptations, etc. The struggle to resist the temptation to masturbate is a struggle that is experienced by every adolescent and every child, without exception. All the elements of the reactionary man's structure are developed in this struggle. It is in the lower middle classes that this structure is reinforced and embedded most deeply. [*The Mass Psychology of Fascism*, p. 55]

What perspective flows from this analysis? What policies and concrete political initiatives must be implemented? The conclusion that you have drawn, as you informed Comrade Steve Long, is that the Marxist movement must "find a way to channel repressed libidinal drives in a progressive direction…"[29]

---

29 Comrade Brenner, you have a somewhat different programmatic agenda, as you inform us in your Utopia document that: "Leaving aside the feasibility (or desirability) of guaranteeing orgasm, there remains a

No one is stopping either of you from devoting your time and energy to this mission. But the International Committee has no interest whatever in participating in this dubious and disoriented project.

21. Eros and Death

Perhaps you imagine that you are engaged in something that is terribly daring and original: that you are somehow opening up new vistas of radical thought with your demand that the International Committee adopt a utopian agenda, that we spend more time speculating about the future world and less on accounts of the past and analyses of the present; that we shift our attention from politics to sex, and that we pay less attention to the objective processes of world economy and more to the subjective urges of the individual. In fact, Comrades Brenner and Steiner, there is nothing very original about your proposals. Marxists have heard it all before, and many times.

In an article "On Eros and Death," written by Trotsky in 1908, he recounts a conversation in a Parisian café with a young Russian intellectual, a supporter of the Decadent movement in art, who expressed dismay with the tendency of Marxists to pay too little attention to the subjective feelings of human beings, to their sexual needs and their fear of death. Why did they not pay more homage to the two moments of existence that comprised the exclusive preoccupation of the Decadents: "the ecstasy of the union of two bodies, and the parting of the soul from the body?" These concerns were poorly and too in-

---

vital point here: ending the tyranny of the genitals is as essential as ending the tyranny of economics if a genuinely human existence is to be possible." To comment on this passage would serve only to diminish its comic effect.

frequently addressed by Marxists, the intellectual complained. "At best, historical materialism seeks to explain the origin of this or that social mood (eroticism, mysticism) by the struggle between different forces in society. Whether it does this well or badly, I don't care. But I, to whom you offer your dubious explanations, shall die nevertheless, and as for all the perspectives your historical materialism spreads before me, even if I believe in them for the sake of my spiritual life, I still set them in the perspective of my inevitable death." For these existential problems, the intellectual protested, Marxism had no satisfactory answers. "But what do *you* offer me?" he asked Trotsky. "Objective analysis? Arguments about necessity? Immanent development? The negation of the negation? But all these things are so terribly inadequate, not for my intelligence, but for my will." [*Culture and Revolution in the Thought of Leon Trotsky* (London, 1999), pp. 54-55]

Trotsky, who had just given a lecture attacking the Decadents and their "anarchy of the flesh," began his reply by protesting: "I find it essentially impossible to accept battle on the ground you have chosen. If you please – you are asking me to create, just in passing, a religious doctrine such as would help a member of the intelligentsia to transcend the shell of his individuality and overcome the terror of death and pretentious skepticism, a doctrine capable of linking mystically his 'subconscious,' the soul of his soul, to the great epoch in which we live. But, please excuse me, this would make a mockery of my viewpoint. It would be as if I listened to a scientific lecture on the historical origins of the Bible, and then expected the speaker to tell me on the basis of the Apocalypse the date of the Second Coming. *Mais ce n'est pas mon métier, messieurs,* I could say to you, this is not my job, and that's that." [ibid. p, 57]

As I read your document, Trotsky's conversation with the Decadents comes to mind. You want us to advance proposals for the family of the future, uncover means by which repressed libidinal drives may be released, work out new forms of gender identity, and campaign against the tyranny of genital-centered sexuality. To which the most appropriate reply is, *Mais ce n'est pas mon métier, messieurs!* All this is simply not part of the mission statement of the International Committee of the Fourth International.

22. Objective conditions, science and history

You decry our "search for salvation in Objective Conditions, in Science or History." Permit me to remind you that the word "salvation" is not part of our political vocabulary. The social program does not include salvation; and those who are seeking it should be referred to clergymen of all faiths, who are the specialists in that field.

No doubt, you will protest that your reference to "salvation" is intended ironically, as a polemical thrust against our "objectivism." I understand that very well, but that doesn't alter the fact that your comment reeks of political despair and cynicism. You ought to retrace the process by which, since leaving the Trotskyist movement, you came under the influence of anti-Marxist conceptions so fundamentally opposed to those that first brought you into the Workers League and International Committee in the early 1970s.

Today you sneer at our preoccupation with history.[30] But you were once part of a generation of student youth who

---

30 In what amounts to a complete misreading of Marx and Engels, you begin your document by quoting a well-known passage from *The Holy Family*, in which the founders of Marxism state that "'History' does nothing. It possesses no colossal riches…" You apparently believe that this passage should be read as a rebuke to the emphasis placed by the

joined the Workers League and the International Committee precisely because it was the only movement whose work was based on the lessons of the tragic historical experiences of the 20th century. Amidst the plethora of radical tendencies that were politically active in the era of our political awakening, the International Committee stood out as the only movement that was able to present an analysis of the Vietnam War, the eruptions in American cities, the expanding wave of working class and anti-imperialist struggles, within the context of a broad historical perspective. On what did we base our opposition to Stalinism, Maoism, Social Democracy, and Pabloite revisionism, if not the lessons of history?

The writings of Leon Trotsky armed those of us who joined the Workers League in the early 1970s with an understanding of the fate of the 1917 October Revolution, Bolshevism and the international struggle for socialism. We immersed ourselves in the study of all the great strategic lessons drawn by Trotsky from the Russian Revolution and its aftermath. The study of the protracted crisis of the German workers' movement from the defeat of the *Spartakus* uprising in 1919, to the victory of the fascists in 1933, the British General Strike of 1926, the revolutionary events in China between 1925 and 1927, the struggle of the Left Opposition in the Soviet Union between 1923 and 1933, the disastrous consequences of popular frontism in France and Spain in the 1930s, and

---

International Committee on the study of history. Of course, it is no such thing. Marx and Engels were criticizing the idealistic conceptions of the Left Hegelians, who transformed history into a self-motivating abstract concept, generating out of itself, in the manner of Hegel's Absolute Idea, events that were mere manifestations of the concept's own logically-driven self-negation. For Marx and Engels, the concept of history had to be abstracted from the study of the development of human society. The outcome of the critique of Hegelian idealism by Marx and Engels was the materialist conception of history.

the Moscow Trials – all these immense historical experiences were incorporated into the training of the cadre of the Workers League and the International Committee. Putting aside for a moment all the irreconcilable programmatic differences, what immediately distinguished the cadre of the ICFI from that of all other movements was its preoccupation with history, its intense belief that the past was not dead, but that, to use the words of Faulkner, "It's not even past!" We believed that history lived in the concrete form of the political conditions and contradictions inherited from the past, and within whose framework the present struggles developed, as well as in the forms of political and social consciousness among the masses.

But now you write as if you find our continued preoccupation with history a cause for bemusement! While you tell us that postmodernism is a mere fad that is on the wane, your own dismissive attitude toward history bears the mark of this reactionary school of bourgeois philosophy.

As for your dismissive reference to science, we see this as an expression of your capitulation to the irrationalist, anti-science and anti-technology moods that are to be found among broad sections of the ex-radical petty-bourgeoisie. We have already dealt with the philosophical roots and implications of this outlook. Let us now consider its practical connotations. In this context, it should be noted that Geoghegan's book included a chapter devoted to the "utopianism" of the late Rudolf Bahro, the East German dissident who eventually emigrated to the German Federal Republic and became active in the newly formed Green Party. Perhaps out of embarrassment, you chose to avoid reference to Geoghegan's sympathetic review of the work of Bahro, who explicitly rejected both Marxism and the central historical role of the working class. He explains that Bahro "rejects the technological/industrial idea of progress which is dominant in the modern world.

It is a selfish and destructive concept which helps perpetuate all the other types of oppression in society. A break has to be made with such ways – future society will have to be 'simpler' or it will not be able to exist at all…" [*Marxism and Utopia*, op. cit., p. 118]

These views are, in fact, very close to those presented by you, Comrade Brenner, in your neo- (or pseudo-) utopian manifesto, *To Know a Thing is to Know its End*. Criticizing Comrade Beams for emphasizing the progressive potential of technology in a socialized economy, which will allow an immense expansion in the productivity of labor and the realization of human potential, you asserted that "A socialist vision, as opposed to a utilitarian one, subordinates productivity to human development, and that means support for ideas that often run directly counter to the maximization of economic growth, ideas like 'the right to be lazy.'"

You were not talking simply about the misuse of technology and human productivity in an economic system dominated by private ownership of the means of production, whose aim is the attainment of maximum profits and the accumulation of massive personal wealth for members of the ruling elite. You state that "there is no reason why … freedom requires endless economic growth," and then add: "The point is rather that, for the first generations after a revolution – whose priorities at any rate will be the elimination of global hunger, poverty and disease – the emphasis will not be so much on technological change as on consolidation, on sorting out what best meets human needs and what works best ecologically."

It boggles the mind to work through the social implications of a freeze, spanning several generations, on economic growth and the *forced* inhibition of technological change [for restraints on the development of technology would require nothing less than police-state measures]. This is a recipe for social catastrophe, inklings of which can be found in the horrifying consequences of the reactionary experiments of various Maoist-influenced movements that were able to come to power. Such views and policies are hostile to Marxism, which, as Trotsky explained in *Revolution Betrayed*, "sets out from the development of technique as the fundamental spring of progress, and constructs the communist program upon the dynamic of the productive forces." [Detroit, 1991, p. 39]

Your effort to separate human freedom from the growth of technique and productivity betrays an ignorance of theory and history. If you were correct, the socialist revolution would represent the first occasion in history when society overthrew its existing forms of economic organization in order to restrain the development of technology and the productivity of labor. But as Trotsky wrote, "Reduced to its primary basis, history is nothing but a struggle for an economy of working time. Socialism could not be justified by the abolition of exploitation alone: it must guarantee society a higher economy of time than is guaranteed by capitalism. Without the realization of this condition, the mere removal of exploitation would be but a dramatic moment without a future." [ibid. p. 68]

As has now become clear, your cynical reference to our confidence in the potential of science betrays a social perspective that is backward, if not outright reactionary.[31]

---

31 There is another aspect of this question that deserves to be considered. The fight for socialist consciousness, above all in the United States, demands an unrelenting defense of scientific thought against all forms of backwardness. This issue was addressed at a lecture that I delivered in New York, in April 2005, on the subject of Terry Schiavo:

> An essential component of efforts to organize workers politically as a class is the struggle to raise their intellectual and cultural level, to champion the cause of scientific thought against all forms of religious superstition and backwardness—that is, to champion a materialist Marxist understanding of not only the socioeconomic

Finally, we come to your contemptuous reference to our conviction that "objective conditions" will provide the foundations for the solution of all political tasks. May we ask, where else are they to be found? In a sentence that you have intended to be a criticism of the International Committee, but which unintentionally exposes your own descent into subjective idealism and irrationalism, you write: "The more the real problems of fighting for socialist consciousness recede over the horizon of 'objective conditions,' the more remote the working class becomes from the activity and concerns of the movement." This

---

relations of society, but also the foundations and structure of human consciousness. As in the past, the socialist movement must recognize the vast scope of its theoretical and pedagogical responsibilities to the working class.

We can draw great encouragement from the fact that science is providing the socialist movement with a vast new array of intellectual weapons. It is ironic that the field of science at the very center of the Terri Schiavo controversy—neurobiology—is the scene today of the most spectacular theoretical breakthroughs. Astonishing advances are being made in the understanding of the physiology of the brain, the most complex of all material structures. And these, in turn, substantiate the materialist understanding of consciousness and cognition championed by Marxism. It is no wonder that the ruling elite should so fear the work of the finest scientists, whose discoveries in the field of neurobiology and related areas of research are systematically demolishing the last redoubts of religious mysticism.

The working class cannot advance without the aid of science. But science itself requires the advance of the working class. Today, the growth of political reaction in the United States places the scientific researcher under siege. But the isolated scientist cannot defend him- or herself any more successfully than the individual worker. In the final analysis, the progress of science as a whole, not to mention the physical safety of individual researchers, depends on the resurgence of a new revolutionary movement of the working class. In the most profound historical sense, the socialist movement unites under its banner both the pursuit of scientific truth in all its forms and the struggle for human equality.

is mysticism, not Marxism. Those who propose to wage their fight for consciousness "over the horizon of 'objective conditions'" are, in fact, seeking to flee reality.

We live and fight in the world of "objective conditions," which is both the source of our present-day troubles as well as their ultimate solution. Whatever shall emerge in the future shall be the product of conditions that exist today. As Marx and Engels explained:

> …in reality and for the *practical* materialist, i.e., the communist, it is a question of revolutionizing the existing world, of practically coming to grips with and changing the things found in existence …
>
> Communism is not for us a *state of affairs* which is to be established, an *ideal* to which reality [will] have to adjust itself. We call communism the *real* movement which abolishes the present state of things. The conditions of this movement result from the now existing premise. [*Marx-Engels Collected Works*, Volume 5 (New York, 1976), pp. 38-49, emphasis in the original]

The understanding that this world, in which we live today, contains within it the real potential for a social revolution that will cleanse the world of all violence and inhumanity is a source of a genuine optimism that has no need for supplementary pseudo-utopian anti-depressants.

* * * * *

The views that you, Comrades Steiner and Brenner, have presented in your various documents record the immense theoretical and political distance that you have drifted from Marxism since you both left the movement nearly three decades ago. To continue along your present trajectory can lead only to the complete repudiation of whatever remains of the political convictions that you espoused many years ago. We hope this will not happen. The International Committee urges both of you to study this document carefully and to reconsider the positions you now hold.

Yours fraternally,
David North
Chairman, International Editorial Board
World Socialist Web Site

Detroit, June 28, 2006

Index